199

MISTAKES
NEW COLLEGE
PROFESSORS
MAKE AND HOW TO
PREVENT THEM

Insider Secrets to Avoid Classroom Blunders

KIMBERLY SARMIENTO

199 Mistakes New College Professors Make and How to Prevent Them: Insider Secrets to Avoid Classroom Blunders

Copyright © 2016 Atlantic Publishing Group, Inc.
1405 SW 6th Avenue • Ocala, Florida 34471 • Phone **352-622-1825** • Fax 352-622-1875
Web site: www.atlantic-pub.com • E-mail: sales@atlantic-pub.com
SAN Number: 268-1250

Library of Congress Cataloging-in-Publication Data

Sarmiento, Kimberly, 1975-
   199 mistakes new college professors make and how to prevent them : insider secrets to avoid classroom blunders / by Kimberly Sarmiento.
      pages cm
   Includes bibliographical references and index.
   ISBN 978-1-60138-965-7 (alk. paper) -- ISBN 1-60138-965-5 (alk. paper) 1. College teachers--Handbooks, manuals, etc. 2. College teaching--Handbooks, manuals, etc. I. Title. II. Title: One hundred and ninety-nine mistakes new college professors make and how to prevent them.
   LB2331.S27 2015
   378.1'25--dc23
                              2015015271

Printed in the United States

Over the years, we have adopted a number of dogs from rescues and shelters. First there was Bear and after he passed, Ginger and Scout. Now, we have Kira, another rescue. They have brought immense joy and love not just into our lives, but into the lives of all who met them.

We want you to know a portion of the profits of this book will be donated in Bear, Ginger and Scout's memory to local animal shelters, parks, conservation organizations, and other individuals and nonprofit organizations in need of assistance.

– Douglas & Sherri Brown,
President & Vice-President of Atlantic Publishing

AUTHOR DEDICATION

I believe that college is a place to discover yourself and your future, and it is OK to take a winding path from what you think will be your major to what you ultimately pursue as your career. Every professor that helps a student along that path will make an impact on that person's life.

I dedicate this book to all the professors who have inspired me, challenged me, and helped mold my future – from my community college drama teacher to my first journalism instructor. I also want to specifically honor the University of Florida's College of Journalism and Department of Political Science. Some of my best memories were made at that campus, and I am so very proud to be a Gator for life!

TABLE OF CONTENTS

Chapter 12: Grading 135

Chapter 13: Managing Distractions 149

High-Tech Distractions.................................. 150

Chapter 14: Overcoming Outside Challenges to Learning 155

Chapter 27: Impressing Office Staff & Your Boss ...257

Chapter 28: Final Thoughts 263

Bibliography 267

Contributors 269

Author Biography 271

Index 273

INTRODUCTION

"The mediocre teacher tells, the good teacher explains, the superior teacher demonstrates, and the great teacher inspires," said William A. Ward, a poet, inspirational writer, and man of great faith. Ward pointed out what separated the teachers people remembered and loved from those who did not inspire their students in the classroom.

Inspirational quotes like this are really what all teachers and professors want to concentrate on. The flip side of the coin is the rather demoralizing idea that "Those who can, do, and those who cannot, teach." If you have decided to pursue a career in academia, the last thing you want to think about is how your former classmates, friends, or even family only think you are teaching because you could not cut it in the corporate world.

The first thing you need to do is put those negative preconceptions about teaching out of your head. You also might want to put aside your dream of changing the world by opening the eyes of your co-eds for the first time. While it is an admirable goal, it could also lead to discouragement, disillusionment, and exhaustion.

As a first-year teacher, whether or not you are able to inspire your students will likely be determined by a combination of your personality and passion as well as a strategic effort to avoid common teaching mistakes. This book cannot help you bring things to your classroom that are not intrinsically you, but it is dedicated to help you learn from seasoned teachers and professors who once stood in your shoes.

The first thing you must understand about teaching is that it should be a calling, not just a profession. You have probably heard the saying "Love what you do and never work a day in your life." My advice, that teaching should be a calling and not just a job, is not about any relatively false philosophy such as this. I love being a writer. My work spans several different genres, such as journalism, business, academia, technical and career development, and yet, I can assure you that there are days when my job is difficult.

Having first-hand teaching experience as a teaching assistant at the University of Florida and an Adjunct Professor at Cameron University in Lawton, Oklahoma, I can assure you that there will be days when teaching feels like the hardest and most unappreciated profession around, no matter how much you love it (nurses will, of course, vie for this title, but I believe it is a tight contest). "It is long hours and hard work, but it is all for the benefit of the students," says Sara Razaire of Volusia County Schools.

As a professor, people will look at you as if your job is not **that** hard. You will hear comments about how you have more time off than other professions (all those banker's holidays and an entire summer to kick back and relax!), and they will measure your work day by how many hours you spend in the classroom. They will not take into account the work you spend grading, researching, writing, working with students individually, on material preparation, or on test development.

In addition to the general public, and perhaps even your friends failing to understand how hard your job is, how much time you spend at it, and how little money you really make early on (this is especially true if you are trying to support a family as an adjunct professor), many people cannot even begin to imagine lecturing to dozens or even hundreds of students day in and day out.

If you are a PhD, you might earn a little more respect with your title than your counterparts who teach elementary or high school students. Regardless, your job will still be plagued with students who did not get the grade they wanted. They will be complaining at your door after every major test and especially at the end of the semester. You will hear about previously unknown learning disabilities and other challenges when the student's grade results in a lower score than usual. You will also have to navigate potentially litigious waters as you avoid a student's unhappiness over a grade turning into something more serious.

This is not the recipe for a job someone gets because they cannot figure out what else to do. **This is the formula for a calling.**

If you are called, then this book is dedicated to making your initial foray into the profession of teaching as easy as possible. As the title denotes, this researched guide compiles 199 mistakes you should avoid as you embark on your new career in academia. Some of these mistakes might seem obvious, whereas others may be actions and attitudes you have not even considered.

PART ONE

CLASSROOM MANAGEMENT & DISCIPLINE

After completing your education (be it your master's degree, PhD, or anything but your dissertation), serving as a teaching assistant is a great way to get your feet wet. Sometimes, it can even lead to developing and instructing your own course at your alma mater while you complete your dissertation. Between both responsibilities, you had sent your résumé to multiple universities with great zeal. Then, after several interviews at different schools, crossing your fingers that the job offer wouldn't get delayed because of hiring freezes at the state level, you eventually received an offer to teach at a wonderful school, and prepared yourself for the beginning of your journey in academia.

As excited as you are to start your teaching career, you are likely full of questions and concerns, which led you to this book. During your first year of teaching, and throughout your career even, there are much more than 199 mistakes you can make. A few you should simply accept and learn from because they will make you a better teacher. Others you will want to forget altogether.

The first thing you want to realize is you are the manager when you stand in front of your class. And even though you may not be working in a corporate environment, it is very important for you maintain "command" of your classroom. Therefore, the very first mistake you should avoid is… **Not thinking of yourself as a manager or leader.** I have witnessed fabulous teachers at work who always held control over their classrooms. I believe this is necessary to your success as a teacher, so this section is dedicated to answering questions you may have on student management and discipline.

CHAPTER 1
Leadership Strategies for Teachers

You will be surprised at just how important maintaining control and discipline are to your success as a teacher, even if you do not think of yourself as a leader just yet. You may even notice the need for a college professor to maintain both actions in his or her classroom already.

"But I am teaching adults," you say. "Certainly they will behave better than a rowdy bunch of teenagers."

Almost certainly your students will behave in a more adult manner than their teenage counterparts in high school. However, do not be surprised if you no longer think of them as adults by the end of your first semester. Some college students are completely responsible for themselves, working to pay their own rent, responsible for all of their own bills (and laundry!), and operating without a safety net at home. Other college students are living in a bubble where they have more privileges than they did in high school, but little more responsibility.

Ergo, at some colleges, you will find yourself taking on more of a manager or mentor role than you might initially realize. Of course, you will have older students as well, and you can probably count on them to be your most responsible co-eds. But overall, even if you want to think of your students as being mature adults many of them are not.

Therefore, you will need to detail out policies about attendance, tardiness, electronic devices, and other issues you might not presently be anticipating. You might be surprised how rudely students will walk in and out of your classroom, even in the middle of a lecture when the exit requires them walking by you to leave. Some will do so without warning. Frankly, this is the kind of behavior that makes you want to offer a "pop" quiz immediately after the student leaves. But that is not the main point of this chapter.

The bottom-line of this section is that whether or not you consider yourself a natural-born leader, you will need to tap into managerial skills in order to maintain control of your classroom and receive the respect you deserve. To do so, you must find within you the ability to stand in front of your students and command their attention.

I was in my late 20s when I worked as an adjunct professor for a mid-sized university in Oklahoma located near a military base. As a result, I found myself not just teaching 18-22 year-olds, but also men and women who had been working on their degrees for more than a decade. At least half of my students were older than me, and I was – on more than one occasion – confused for a fellow student on the first day of class. Yet I was still their teacher, and I had to make them believe I deserved both their respect and their recognition as an expert in my field.

As a first-year teacher, assuming you followed a traditional route through college, you could be as little as four or five years older than your students. That does not mean they will not respect you, but you should take care to avoid mistakes that could undermine your authority and make managing your classroom harder than it needs to be. This chapter is dedicated to helping you recognize and bypass those errors.

What is Your Management Style?

There are many different types of leaders in the world. In fact, ask a room full of people to name a great leader and you hear the names of government officials, military generals, corporate executives, and even sport icons. They may have little in common, except that they all led a group of people to achieve something that brought them recognition in the process.

How they led varies dramatically, from an autocratic style where the manager makes decisions unilaterally to democratic leaders who empower their followers to make decisions by majority. While you might feel uncomfortable thinking of yourself as an autocrat, I am sure you can see that leading by vote would be a poor idea in your classroom.

As you decide what leadership tools and techniques you feel comfortable employing in your classroom, consider the following advice:

MISTAKE 1
Letting students direct your class...

You do not need to be oppressive or militaristic, but you do need to manage the activity of the classroom. You need to be the one that controls the lecture, discussion, and pace at which you cover the material. Doing this successfully will require planning, analysis, resourcefulness, and flexibility. For you to meet the needs of your students, cover the required curriculum, and ensure you are seen as the leader of your class, you need to plan ahead while monitoring your class's performance to identify needed adjustments.

It is acceptable for a student to ask a question that leads the class off on an educational tangent every now and then, but you need to recognize when to bring the class back to the original topic. You can achieve this by making sure the tangent subject ties in with the material you need to cover or simply by tabling the discussion to a later date and returning to the original material.

In order to ensure that your students are not leading you off topic too often, measure your progress against your lesson plans. If you find that you are not covering your planned curriculum on a regular basis, you might need to make sure you – not your students – are setting the tone for your class.

MISTAKE 2
Not setting goals for your students…

"Before you are a leader, success is all about growing yourself. When you become a leader, success is all about growing others," said Jack Welch, former CEO of General Electric. Welch grew GE into a Fortune 500 Company and mentored countless future business leaders along the way.

I do not know what potential your students hold within them, but I do know that you should set goals for their development that extend beyond scoring well on a standardized test. Giving your students an objective – be it individual or group – is beneficial on multiple levels. Having a goal helps engage students on a higher level and establishes you as their leader to guide them in achieving their objectives.

A goal for your students could be to challenge each of them to improve their graded performance a certain percentage from one test to another.

It could also be that if they write in-class essays particularly well, you will leave essay questions off an exam. I believe it is especially helpful to give students who struggle in your subject matter goals for improvement. If you can train the student to focus on improvement rather than just their letter grade, you can help them fulfill their potential – whatever that might be.

MISTAKE 3

Being too relaxed...

A portion of this book will address mistakes you can make when disciplining your class, but it is important to remember that another discipline mistake can be having no standard of discipline at all. There is a phrase saying that many first-year teachers do not understand until it is too late: "Do not let them see you smile until Christmas."

You are probably wondering why in the world you would want to come across so harsh early on, but the idea is simple – start tough because it is far easier to relax than it is to regain control if you have lost it.

Have a plan for discipline that complies with your school standards and is well communicated to your students. Be prepared to reiterate several times at the beginning of the school year and follow through with it early so students believe that you mean what you say. Remember that making idle threats will not help you build respect. You might think you are being merciful or helping them learn the new system, but in fact, you are teaching them that they can get away with breaking your rules to an extent. Instead, make sure you back up your words with deeds.

MISTAKE 4
Wanting to be everyone's favorite professor...

For the majority of the individuals reading this book, one thing might be true – you want your students to like you. You probably even want them to love you. Go ahead and admit that and get it out of the way. This book covers 199 mistakes new teachers make and how to avoid them, but wanting to be liked too much is probably at the top of most "Do Not" lists for teachers and professors everywhere.

Wanting to be liked could cause you to be too lax in terms of discipline. It could lead you to use too many "fun" activities in class and not communicate the lesson as well. While you may not want to think of them this way, your students can sense weakness in their supposed leaders. If your students believe they can manipulate you or guilt you because of your desire to be well-liked, this could cause you to lose control of your classroom without even realizing it.

Of course, you do not need to come to the conclusion that the inverse is true – that if wanting to be well-liked is a weakness, not caring what your students think must be a strength. No. If you come across as completely unfeeling or uncaring, you will not be able to create a bond with the students, which could make it more difficult for you to engage them in learning. You should not strive to be hated, just like you should not let your co-eds walk all over you just so you will be loved.

If you were inspired to teach because of your favorite professor(s) or because some movie inspired you to make a difference in the lives of your students, being loved by your students probably matters to you a great deal. Even if you have other motives for teaching, you still probably want to be liked by your students – after all, that does making teaching easier and more productive. And of course, it can only help your career to score highly on student evaluation surveys, right?

The most important thing for you to remember as a new professor is that being loved or liked cannot be your number one objective. You need to earn your student's respect and admiration and being liked – or even loved – will naturally follow. Plan your classroom activities to foster an atmosphere of learning and success rather than "fun," and you will make an impact on the students that will last. Ultimately, you will be remembered for what you taught your students, not how "cool" you were.

MISTAKE 5
Connecting with your students over social media…

Some forms of social media might actually be very advantageous in communicating with your students. For example, using Twitter to update your students on schedule or curriculum changes might prove beneficial to you and your class. However, connecting with your students on a venue such as Facebook – which is designed to be personal in content – might put you in the position of needing to censor yourself.

Many of my closest friends have faced that moment on a social media platform where they find themselves connected to an older family member (parent, aunt, grandparent, etc…) and then they start thinking twice about what they post or comment. That is precisely why in terms of career management, I advise clients not to connect with professional associates on Facebook. Instead, I encourage them to connect on professional networking sites such as LinkedIn and maintain different tones on each platform.

I would suggest new professors take a similar approach. You should connect with fellow professors, administrative staff, and students on sites such as LinkedIn, and allow them to follow a carefully crafted messaging site such as Twitter. Leave social media outlets where you upload pictures and comment on political and social issues (such as Facebook) to more personal contacts.

CHAPTER 2
The Importance
of Professionalism

Remember that the closer you are to your students in age, the more you will need to use an aura of professionalism to distinguish yourself as their teacher and not their peer. Assuming you are a new graduate, you may not have spent a great deal of time in a corporate environment. If that is the case, you might not realize how important it is to dress, speak, and present yourself in a professional manner. You may not even know what that means.

Professionalism for teachers means remembering that you are the leader of the classroom and you are NOT your students' friend. You – or one of your friends – might have experimented with your physical appearance a bit in college and got a tattoo, a few piercings, or dyed your hair an unnatural color. Whatever the case, now that you are professional you may be expected to remove, change, or cover up those experiments that were once considered expressions of your personality.

It might seem unfair that this is expected of you, but remember, perception often becomes reality. If you are perceived by students, colleagues, or administration as unprofessional or a "bad fit" for the culture, you may not keep your job very long.

What might seem even more unfair is as a new hire, you might not have the same opportunities that tenured professors seem to have. I can still remember one economics professor at UF who most certainly did not look the part of a financial expert. But he was tenured – and an awesome professor – so he could wear jeans with holes in them any time he wanted.

You need to "dress to impress" and work hard to create an aura of professional distinction until you have secured your place on campus.

MISTAKE 6
Letting students call you by your first name…

While it is probably not a good idea for any college professor to allow their undergraduate students to call them by their first name, it is even less wise if you are young. In the U.S., we are not as formal as other cultures in this regard; however, addressing someone by his or her first name denotes a level of familiarity that should not be present between teacher and student.

Thinking back to how you spoke to your teachers and college professors, there was most likely a difference between how you spoke to them versus how you addressed your friends. If you believe your students would benefit from a more relaxed learning environment, meaning you allow them to address you by your first name, then pay attention to how your colleagues are addressed by their students. Try to imagine if this approach would earn you the same respect as your colleagues. If the answer is no, then adjust your strategy accordingly.

When teaching graduate students, you might think you can relax this rule a bit, but that might not be the case. As I was completing my master's degree, I watched several PhD candidates struggle with how to address professors they worked closely with on a daily basis. To this day, there are professors who I still remember as "Dr. So-and-So" rather than "Steve."

One strategy you can use for this rule is to pay attention to how tenured professors refer to each other when talking to students. If they commonly call each other by their title and last name, they are probably reinforcing an idea of authority rather than familiarity in the department. If that is the case, you should follow their lead and adopt a more formal tone with your students. If your colleagues seem to communicate in a more informal manner, you can follow suit, but do not feel like you have to. It still might be a good idea to not be too familiar with your students until you have earned a more solid position on campus.

I struggled myself having people refer to me as "Mrs. Sarmiento" in my late 20s. Therefore, I can understand your discomfort. However, it might be equally as important for you to set yourself apart and use a formal title as it is for your students to see you as the authority figure in the room. Just remember that while you can always ask a student down the road to call you by your first name, it would be a little awkward to ask a student to switch to a more formal method of communication once a casual relationship is established.

MISTAKE 7
Not being mindful of your appearance...

Having worked with dozens of career coaches, I can promise you that appearance matters in interviews. In fact, given how little a hiring manager can really learn about you during an interview, appearance and how you present yourself might be the leading factor in whether or not you get the job.

"Seeing is believing" is an idiom that dates back hundreds of years. The idea is that tangible proof is necessary for belief and trust. However, we have come to think of it as also meaning that people will believe what they see. Therefore, no matter how much we rage against the shallowness of being judged merely on our looks, the simple truth is that appearance matters.

Being mindful of your appearance does not just mean being clean and well put-together; it also means presenting the correct image to those around you. The good news is that you do not need to look like an airbrushed movie star on the cover of a magazine to ensure your continued employment. However, dressing (and looking) like your students expect adults/authority figures to dress (and look) is an important consideration when seeking to establish yourself as the leader of your classroom.

To this day, two of my high school teachers stand out in my memory for their appearance. One looked like she came straight out of the movie *Grease 2* with tight sweaters stretched over an ample bosom and big, bleach blonde hair. The other teacher was an older woman who was eccentric in her taste to say the least. In these instances, being unusual did not cost them respect, but being overly "sexy" did. It might be unfair, but it is reality.

Again, as you establish yourself as the leader of your classroom, make sure you look the part. If you are unsure what is acceptable and what is not, turn again to your colleagues and use them as your guide. And definitely make sure you understand the school dress code for students, and govern yourself accordingly – you will do yourself no favors by wearing something that a student would only wear to a club or, conversely, to re-paint their apartment.

MISTAKE 8

Using contemporary slang...

As a writer who was born in the 1970's, I learned to use email, text, and social media as an adult. Ergo, I am mostly in the dark when it comes to the abbreviated slang that is quickly turning into another language among the tech-savvy generation that followed mine. I'll admit, my love for words and grammar causes me to suffer great pain when others around me slaughter the English language.

So having fully admitted my bias, I am still going to advise you to stay away from slang when you lecture your students. Use of the occasional phrase to emphasize a point is acceptable, but one of the greatest ways you can establish your qualifications is to simply "sound" smart. You do not do so by using frequent slang, vulgarity, or "text talk." And for the sake of all that is good in the world, do not say "hash tag" as you stand in front of your class and lecture. Other than to illicit a potential laugh, saying phrases like "hash tag Civil War," "hash tag racist South," "hash tag go freedom" will do little to impress your audience.

Of course I realize that every generation has words that seep into their vernacular so extensively that they no longer recognize the words as being slang. Be careful to do this as little as possible, if for no other reason than to set a good example for your students. After all, you can hardly expect them to speak or write any better than you do in your lectures. Whatever standard you have for your students, set it higher for yourself.

MISTAKE 9

Fraternizing with students...

In college, when students and professors are all adults, the lines of fraternization can blur. You might find yourself frequenting the same establishments or cheering on your school's team at the same events. However, you need to create and maintain strong boundaries for socialization with your students. When you are old enough to have a child the same age as your students, you might have to alternate between the role of parent and teacher, but until that is the case, you should strive to been seen as your students' teacher both in and out of the classroom.

If you are part of the same social circles as some of your students or somehow see your students in other social settings, do not get comfortable and tell them to call you "Jim." If you see your students at a football game or another sports outing, parade, concert, or other community event, treat them as if they are still your student and maintain your professionalism.

While it is understandable that you want to relax and "be yourself" when you leave the classroom, you should be mindful of that fact that when you attend school functions or events, where a great number of students might be present, you will also make an impression on your co-eds. You do not want to undo all the work you have established in the classroom with one visit outside the classroom.

MISTAKE 10
Dating or sleeping with a student...

You will most likely find a wide-range of policies and rules regarding professor-and-student relationships when you are hired. However, whether it is permissible or not, it is generally not a good idea to date a student you currently teach or could potentially teach in the future.

There is a strong chance that you will be close in age to some of your students. In fact, when I was teaching at Cameron University in Oklahoma, some of my classes were mostly composed of military personnel or their spouses. This meant that many of my students were my age or older. If your first job is at a community college, you might experience a similar scenario.

Despite the fact that you and your students are probably all legal adults 18 years old or older, it is still not a good idea to date or have sexual relations with a student.

If you find yourself attracted to a student and believe the feeling is mutual, the best option would be to wait until the student has graduated to begin a relationship. If you are teaching upperclassmen or graduate-level students, this might seem unnecessary, but remember that your relationship is not one between equals if you have authority over them as his or her professor. Therefore, if you do not wait for the person to graduate before you start a relationship, at least make sure he or she never takes a course from you.

The risk of dating a student in one of your courses is more than just the fact that it might violate university policy or appear unprofessional. There is additional risk that you are showing favoritism, which can lead to accusations of sexual harassment. The damage that can be done to your career if this type of relationship ends badly is not worth whatever reward you might think will come from it.

Things to keep in mind when considering even a consensual relationship between student and faculty:

- The inherit inequity in the relationship if you hold grading power over the student.

- The possibility that some people will believe the student did not earn the grade they received if/when the relationship becomes public.

- If the relationship is kept secret, the student's academic performance could come into question after the fact.

- If the relationship ends badly, you could be accused of sexual harassment or negatively impacting the student's grade, regardless of how impartial you remained.

- Your reputation could be damaged if the student talks about you during or after the relationship; this is particularly perilous early in your career.

If these warnings are insufficient for you to err on the side of caution and avoid these types of relationships, consider that in early 2015, Harvard University decided to ban sexual relationships between faculty and undergraduates for the first time, and significantly strengthen language in its policies pertaining to sexual misconduct (**www.npr.org 2015**).

Harvard is just one of many U.S. colleges that has decided to strengthen and reinforce its policies on professor-student relationships. For example, Arizona State University has recently joined the group of college institutions that prohibit these types of relationships on their campuses to avoid the accusations and drama that can happen if a professor-student relationship ends badly. These changes are most likely in response to the demand for schools to strengthen their efforts to prevent sexual abuse, and help victims of harassment and rape.

And though there is a more gray area when dealing with graduate students, it is not a free and clear space either. All of the same concerns listed above still apply – particularly the feeling that it is an act of sexual harassment when an older professor hits on a younger graduate student. Even if your ages are more closely aligned, you still might not want to risk negative appearances this early in your career.

"When a grad student and faculty member start sleeping together, rarely is it a well-kept secret; often, the student becomes a department pariah. Without support from fellow students (and, often, dismissed by the other professors in the department), many of these once-promising grad students wind up out of the discipline entirely. (Schuman 2014)."

Try to remember this perception and keep in mind that you might not only hurt your student's reputation, but your own, too, along with your chances of making tenure.

MISTAKE 11
Mixing it up with the class clown...

If you are a bit of a jokester yourself, you might be tempted to play along when a student starts cracking jokes or clowning around. It is certainly fine to tell some jokes and make your students laugh from time to time. However, you also need to maintain an aura of professionalism that lets the students know you are NOT "one of them."

I know as a professor you want to be liked (well, some of you do), and you might even be one of those adults that find "burping" and "farting" noises funny. On some occasions, your "clown" might even crack some very funny jokes. You may smile, but you should be cautious not to get caught up in the laughter of the classroom. It will be hard enough to regain control of a bunch of raucous teens or 20-somethings once the giggles take hold, and it will not be easier if you are busy having a good belly laugh as well.

Also, if one of your students cracks a joke that might be considered "at your expense," you should be sure not to respond and use them as the "punch line." You should be made of thicker skin than your students can hope to muster. Do not take any of their jokes or comments personally, and make sure you maintain the aura of a leader at all times.

Finally, be cautious of unintended connotations connected to some jokes. Ensure that any joke you make does not have any negative gender, racial, or religious stereotypes included. Young adults can be highly sensitive, so it is best to err on the side of caution and not risk offending anyone.

MISTAKE 12
Responding harshly to a disrespectful student...

Every generation has their "walked two miles to school, in the snow, uphill, both ways" stories. I believe another version of that is "If I said/did that, my parents would have...." Nevertheless, it is a common perception today that teens and young adults are more pampered, more disrespectful, and tend to use more swear words and other vulgarities that would get you fired if you repeated such language.

If that perception is correct, the probability that you might have a student or two talk back to you, or perhaps even curse at you, seems far higher than when you were a student. There is a possibility that you might have an angry student get belligerent with you in class, thinking that they have the floor to say whatever they please. When a student speaks to you in this manner, it could be tempting to speak back to them in the same way to put them in their place per se; however, you should resist that urge.

When a student is disrespectful, you should remain calm, professional, and above all else, in control. Whatever your policy is to deal with disruptive students, put those procedures into practice. Ask the student to leave immediately if you feel that they are too disruptive to the class. If they refuse, you can call security. If you feel it has not gone that far, simply instruct the student to sit down, be quiet, and inform him or her that you will discuss the issue with them in greater detail at a later time.

Just be careful not to yell, curse, or insult the student in your efforts to establish yourself as the dominant person in the room. You want to maintain control of the classroom and of your emotions. Doing so will ensure that the non-disruptive students respect you while showing the disrespectful student that he or she is not going to get under your skin or provoke you.

MISTAKE 13
Responding emotionally to a personal attack…

During all the preparation you have done to get ready for your first teaching job, it may have never occurred to you that a student might insult you on a personal level. If a student gets upset, angry, hurt, or frustrated, then they might say something mean or hurtful to you. They could potentially bring your race, gender, political affiliation, or religion into question, and turn these characteristics into a blame-game for your teaching methods. Recognizing that this is a possibility and preparing for it ahead of time could help you keep your cool and maintain a professional demeanor in the face of a painful verbal attack.

It seems that the Internet and online comment options have emboldened people to say things they would have usually never voiced out loud. This used to be done anonymously on message boards or blogs, but now people will leave obnoxious, over-the-top comments with their names attached. Of course, the next evolution is for people to now say the unthinkable straight to other people's faces. You could hear simple insults such as you are ugly, fat, or old, or more vulgar comments from students who are better at insulting you than you could have ever imagined. If this situation arises, you must maintain a level of professionalism that shows the student is not getting to you in the least.

First, you need to resist the urge to internalize the comments and wonder if the five pounds you have gained is starting to show or obsess about a blemish you saw in the mirror that morning. The student lashing out at you does not have an opinion you should concern yourself with. You need to focus on the people who decide the status of your employment, because losing your cool in these types of situations will not impress them.

So, to recap, do not take insults personally. It is far more likely that a student's insults are a reflection of their inability to do their work or frustration over not understanding a concept. While young adults might be good talkers, they are not necessarily good communicators. They very well could lack the ability to determine what is upsetting them and address it properly. Instead, they will lash out and try to hurt someone else to distract themselves from feelings of inadequacy. Many of your students will outgrow this after a couple of semesters on campus. Sadly, some adults will never grow out of this habit. This is something you must accept and deal with.

Even if you do take their comments personally on some level, do not show it. Responding emotionally to a student would damage your image of being in control of your classroom and could cause other students to lose respect for you. The best response is for you to maintain your self-control, and address the student's outburst in a professional manner. If that means asking the student to leave the room, do so in a calm, controlled manner.

Once you have addressed the outburst from the student, feel free to give your class an assignment that will allow you to regain your composure on the inside if you need to. Halt your lecture and give a reading assignment so you can sit at your desk for a moment and calm down internally. The biggest thing you need to achieve is to not let your students know you were shaken. Do not get angry and yell, and do not get hurt and cry.

MISTAKE 14

Overcompensating for your perceived shortcomings...

You have heard of the Napoleon complex, a type of psychological phenomenon that is said to exist in short people where they seek to overcompensate for insecurities caused by their short stature. I have heard of short, female teachers who operated like dictators, because by middle school, their students already started towering over them. On a college campus, a young, short professor might be mistaken for a student. This can be frustrating when trying to establish yourself as the authority in your classroom.

It can happen that these teachers develop terrifying reputations with their students. They were not liked or loved, but feared instead. At a glance, it appears these teachers are taking the philosophy of "speak softly, but carry a big stick" a little too far.

If there is some area that you perceive as being a weak point for you, address it as best you can, but do not let it dominate your concerns. You should work to highlight your strengths rather than worry about covering up your weaknesses. With a good amount of planning and preparation, you can shrink your weaknesses to a point where your students will not notice them.

Understand that your students walk into the classroom assuming you are in charge. While some of them might try to push the boundaries and see if you stand by your regulations, they still walk in expecting you to be the one they need to try to challenge. Automatically, this means they respect you as the "boss" of the class. Your goal is to not lose that respect.

As a new teacher, you might be younger than many of the other teachers and sometimes younger than your students. Do not let that be something that makes you feel insecure. If you maintain your professionalism and do your job well, no one will notice your age before long.

While your students are probably not perceptive enough to realize if you practice a Napoleon complex, or some version thereof, coworkers, supervisors and other professors will notice. If you are too extreme, the very thing you think is keeping the respect of your students might cost you that of your department.

CHAPTER 3
Communications Strategies for Teachers

Your communications strategies might differ based on whether you are teaching a lecture, lab, or discussion in a class setting. Depending on the class setup, you will need to plan how you communicate with your students. If you are instructing a lab, you will be providing more "hands-on" instruction where you will need to go around the classroom and check on your students' work one-on-one. On the other hand, in a large lecture room setting, the only time you interact with your students individually will be in your office hours.

How you convey information to your students is just as important as the reading material you select and the methods you use to evaluate mastery of the subject. While it might seem like your students will score your evaluations in direct relation to the grades they receive in your class, I believe it is how well you communicate that really determines a student's overall impression of your teaching skills. If you are an engaging lecturer who presents material in a dynamic manner that makes a strong impact on the student, I believe they are more likely to rate you positively regardless of the grade they earn in your class. Conversely, if you are dull and boring, a student might rate you poorly, even if they found it easy to make an A in your class.

You might find yourself getting a slight bit of stage fright at the thought of standing and lecturing in front of 50 or more students. If this happens, try to remember your lecturing skills and how much of a direct impact they have on your job. There are things you can do to enhance your communications skills even before you deliver your first presentation, and a bit of planning will hopefully help you avoid getting tongue-tied. Read on for mistakes to avoid in terms of lecturing, presenting, and communicating with your class.

MISTAKE 15
Not using visual aids...

As a recent graduate, chances are that you had few classes where the professor stood in the front of the room and just lectured without overheads, PowerPoint presentations, or other visual aids. In fact, there are all sorts of web tools and applications available to professors today to communicate visually what they want their students to grasp contextually.

To not use any visual aids or take advantage of the technology tools your school may offer you would be a mistake. You should have plenty of audio/visual equipment available to you if you petition for it, and personnel on campus that can help you set it up and use it. If you are unfamiliar with any particular piece of equipment, be sure to seek help from the technical professionals at your school.

If you think a video or image could create controversy for you, despite its ability to communicate what you want to teach, it might be best to avoid using it until you have established yourself on campus better. In another section of this book, I will more completely address the issue of "triggering" that seems to be common at university campuses these days.

However, I believe it is important to keep the idea of avoiding visual aids that could lead to complaints of sexual harassment or bigotry from your students. Even at the most liberal of campuses, it is getting more and more difficult to cover "offensive" material without repercussions. A tenured professor might be able to get away with some questionable content, but as the new person on campus, you should be cautious.

MISTAKE 16
Using words or language your students do not understand...

As a parent, I never engaged in the practice of "baby talk" or talked "down" to my children. However, I did encourage them to ask questions if I used words they did not understand, and was ready to use a synonym to explain a word if my vocabulary exceeded their understanding.

While you want to expand your students' vocabulary – and will undoubtedly do so over the course of the school year – you probably do not have time to stop your lesson every time one of your students does not understand a word or phrase you used.

Also, do not use advanced vocabulary words as a means of establishing yourself as the "smartest person in the room." You can lecture using million-dollar words if you like, but if your students cannot understand anything you are saying because of it, you are wasting your time – and theirs. I am not saying you should "dumb down" college-level text, but your students' should not need to bust out a dictionary to get through your lectures.

If you do not heed this warning, do not be surprised if students stop attending your class. If your communication is ineffective, they might decide to roll the dice and see if they can pass your course by using the textbook and other resources you provided them with. If you want the chance to engage your students in person, do it in a way that they can grasp and understand.

MISTAKE 17
Being unwilling to explain yourself...

Being unwilling to explain yourself to your students – at least a little – will do you little good in terms of earning and keeping their respect.

You are there to teach, and students are there to learn. If you adopt a complete philosophy of "because I said so," you could be failing to instruct your students. That is not to suggest that you need to explain ad nauseam every classroom policy or decision you make. I am only suggesting that when a student asks "why" it is occasionally OK to explain your reasoning to them.

Furthermore, if a student is asking questions about a subject, there might be a misunderstanding in place between you and your students. If a co-ed has failed to understand a lesson or an action from you, letting that continue could damage the learning process.

Do not adopt an attitude of refusing to repeat or explain yourself at all. While you do not want to let your students lead you off course in the middle of a lecture, ensuring that they understand the word or examples you are using is pivotal to communicating your message.

It is understandable that you might not want to allow students to ask questions while you are in the middle of a lecture. Allowing too many questions is a sure way to get derailed and permanently off-topic. If you adopt such a policy, be sure to have a dedicated question- and answer-time before you cover too much material. Also, evaluate how well your students are engaged at several points during a lecture. If you look out at a sea of confused faces, it might be time to back up and make sure your students are grasping your meaning.

MISTAKE 18

Not admitting if you are wrong...

Let us say you had the flu, did not get any sleep, were nearly hit by a poor driver on the way to school, and broke a nail five minutes before your lecture. All together, you have a litany of excuses as to why you suffered the horrible indignity of actually being wrong in front of your class. Still, do not operate as if it did not happen. Correct the error and move on. You are not here to teach your students inaccuracies and misinformation.

MISTAKE 19

Not admitting when you do not know an answer...

Of course you want to be perceived as the foremost authority on all subject matter related to the courses you are teaching. However, there are going to be times during the semester when a student is going to stump you. Rather than trying to stutter through an answer that would be less than complete, you should tell your students you will address that question the next day and then continue on with the material you need to cover during that class period.

Of course, the key to this strategy is to follow through on promises such as these. Students will perceive you as the expert of your subject as long as you do not let questions drop or go unaddressed. Promising them that you will address something later can be seen as good classroom management rather than ignorance. But if you fail to follow through, the student(s) might begin to wonder why you dropped the ball. So, if a student asks you something and you are unsure of the answer, make sure to take note of it and get back to it at a later time.

MISTAKE 20

Using sarcasm...

Alright, if sarcasm is a second language for you, you are not going to like this section much. Heck, it is not my favorite talking point either. In fact, when I first read Katie Hurley's "Want to Stop Mean Girls? Raise Nice Girls, Instead" article and I got to that particular piece of advice, I rolled my eyes.

Then I thought more about what she was saying and I read the article again. Hurley is a Child and Adolescent Psychotherapist and wrote the article about her efforts to start a "friendship club" among fourth grade girls at the school she was working. This was brought on as a response to teachers asking her for help with female students whose relationship troubles with each other were interrupting classroom settings.

The program was successful and one key element she sites is cutting down on "cutting comments" between the girls. If this is effective between elementary-aged children, it will be effective in your effort to relate to your students as well.

First off, students will not always understand your sarcastic comments or that you were attempting to be comedic instead of insulting. This misunderstanding will undoubtedly lead to difficulties as you work to impart your lessons. Whether a student becomes hurt and does not listen to the rest of your lesson, or the student thinks you meant something else entirely, your communications will have failed among one or more of the individuals in your class.

Instead, say what you mean in a clear and concise way. Be patient with a student who is sarcastic or "smart" with you and avoid temptation to respond similarly.

MISTAKE 21
Not setting a discussion boundary...

If you do not let your students know on day one how to speak up in your class, you are not allowing the learning environment to be the best that it can be.

It is important that you set a boundary. For example, if you prefer structured conversation, it is important that you tell your students to raise their hands. If there is a certain time where you do not want to facilitate discussion, let them know. For example, "During this lecture, please jot down any comments or questions, and we will get to those at the end."

On the other hand, if you prefer a more open and natural discussion forum, it is important to let your students know that they can speak whenever they feel the need. For example, "Don't bother raising your hands — be respectful of other people while they are speaking, but if you have a response or question, feel free to speak up."

Different professors prefer different discussion styles; your students have probably experienced several of them by now, so it important to let them know what you expect from them.

This is something that should be discussed either in the syllabus or during the first week of class. If your students are not complying, gently remind them of how your class operates in order to get to the desired discussion setting.

CHAPTER 4
Maintaining Control of Your Classroom

Let us assume that you have already decided what the rules of your classroom are going to be and have outlined your expectations in your syllabus. Now you must address the ever-difficult task of deciding how to discipline your students if the situation arises. Again, you may wonder why you need to "discipline" adults at all. Try to remember that even corporate managers and human resources personnel have to "discipline" company employees. In this case, we are not talking about reprimanding a student per se, but exercising enough discipline to maintain control of your classroom.

In all likelihood, your institution has some sort of student handbook that co-eds are expected to follow. This probably deals with serious offenses such as cheating, plagiarism, fighting, or sexual harassment. You will be expected to defend rules against such behavior, but you have generally accepted expectations and social conventions to back you up.

However, there are smaller offenses that you have to decide how to handle. When a student talks out of turn or causes a disruption in your classroom by clowning around, you must decide if such behavior will earn the student an invitation to leave the room or if you can overlook it and get the class back on the right path. If you are unsure how to handle these situations, do not hesitate to consult your fellow teachers to see what they do in their classrooms. If you watch enough examples and receive good advice, then you will be able to sort out what works best for you.

In the meantime, as you seek to develop your discipline policy, there are some things you should remember NOT to do; these errors range from disciplinary actions you should never use to things that will just give you a headache if you do not avoid them. This chapter is dedicated to covering how to maintain control of your classroom while avoiding a wide-range of disciplinary mistakes.

Ways Not To Discipline – Ever

There are many mistakes you can make your first year of teaching (and even beyond) that may affect you professionally. However, there are a few that will likely get you fired or at least reprimanded by your superiors. It should be your highest priority to avoid committing these mistakes. Read below for the mistakes related to discipline:

MISTAKE 22
Using ridicule to get a student in line…

If you have a sarcastic personality or caustic sense of humor, it would be easy to make snide comments when one of your students gets out of line or responds poorly to a question asked in class. As natural as that is to you, I highly recommend that you avoid engaging students in this manner.

There are several reasons why you should avoid ridiculing a student in class. The first is that it is more likely to cause you to lose control of your classroom than to keep it. Students will laugh at almost any joke you crack – at least all of the ones they understand. When laughter breaks out in your classroom, calming the students down will take some effort. If the students are laughing at another co-ed, what little control you have left will evaporate if the student you ridiculed should react in anger or tears – both of which are possible. Whatever you hoped to achieve with your comment – if you thought about it at all – will probably not be accomplished, and there will be negative results.

The second thing that will happen after a snide comment is that you will seriously damage your professional image among students and parents who hear about the incident. I know you probably do not think you will encounter parents much in a collegiate environment, but it can happen. Ridiculing or embarrassing a student in the classroom is probably a good way to hear from the person paying for that student's education.

The last thing you need to do is allow one small comment to injure your reputation as a professional. If you were working at an office among other adults, you might be able to make a snide comment without consequence if you do not let it happen very often. However, students may not receive the comment well at all and neither will their parents. Once you have lowered their opinion and respect for you, it will be difficult to regain confidence and control of your classroom. Teaching and relationship building will become more challenging, and some students will look for other signs that you are not doing your job well. Basically, you will stack the deck of cards against yourself and make your job harder than it needs to be.

If you are tempted to ridicule a student to keep them from continuing to make fun of or tease another person in your classroom, you should think twice about adopting such tactics. While this might seem like a good way to defend the individual who is being teased and could make the "bully" understand what it is like to be laughed at, it is far more likely that you will only create an atmosphere where you'll continually drag yourself down to a level that should be beneath your character. Once your students start to think of you as being "one of them" or "on their level," you have basically lost your ability to be their leader. In instances such as this, it is far more important for you to set an example of how to handle a "bully" with self-control than to try to put the student in his or her place using ridicule.

In addition to the damage you can do to the relationships you have with your students, you will permanently fail the student you ridiculed. Whatever reason you have for wanting to bring the student back in line with a snide comment, you must not overlook the fact that it is your responsibility to teach all of the students in your classroom. Appropriately disciplining a student who disrupts your teaching allows you to send a message that your instruction is important, and you are not to be interrupted. Ridiculing a student sends another message altogether. It conveys the idea that the lesson is not important, and you are willing to abandon your teaching to talk condescendingly to one of your students. While that student might not act out again, he or she will not likely seek your help if he or she needs it for fear of more ridicule. Furthermore, other students might be equally unlikely to ask for help because they do not want you to make fun of them. This means you have not just damaged your ability to control your classroom; you have decreased your ability to effectively do your job.

Finally, it is not wise to use ridicule or snide comments to try to get a student to perform better academically. If a student answers your question with a snide remark or even an incredibly stupid comment that shows they were not paying attention to what you were saying, your job is to keep your composure and not make the individual feel dumb. As in the above scenario, making a student feel stupid will not just decrease the likelihood that one student will feel comfortable participating in class – it will lower the chances that any of your students will want to respond to your questions.

Furthermore, you must not respond to a question from a student in a snide or negative manner. You may think that the saying "There are no stupid questions" is completely false. There are, in fact, many stupid questions, and you will probably hear dozens of them throughout your first year of teaching. No matter how much a student's question makes you wonder if he or she is even listening to you talk, you cannot answer them in a sarcastic or mean way. You have to remain professional and address questions completely, no matter how tedious this task can be. If you do not adopt this philosophy, your students might stop asking questions – even when they do not understand the material. If they stop asking questions, you might find yourself wondering why they are performing badly on homework and tests. Maintaining an environment that encourages questions and learning will be the key to your success. Do not sabotage yourself with a sarcastic or snide comment – no matter how funny it sounds in your head.

MISTAKE 23
Cursing…

Almost everyone on the planet understands how easy it is to lose your temper and say something you do not mean, especially when it comes to yelling or cursing. Of course, just about everyone who has done this realizes that losing composure with a student or subordinate does not gain you respect or make the student more likely to do as you wish. Simply put, while yelling and/or cursing might seem like a good way to let off steam and let your students know you "mean business" it will still demonstrate poor professionalism.

Whether cursing is acceptable in an office setting varies on the office, the company, the manager, and the curse words that are used. A four-letter word at one company might not get you in trouble, but could land you in sensitivity training at another corporation. Cursing at work could negatively impact the impression you make on your boss or potential clients. When I advise clients in career management, I tell them to completely avoid it in an interview and limit it as much as possible in a new position.

In a school environment, you need to completely remove curse words from your vocabulary – even if your students know more profanities than you do. While your class has probably heard everything you could think to say, it is still the essence of a professional teacher to avoid the use of vulgar language at school.

If a student brings your foul language or vulgarity to your boss's attention, you will almost certainly earn yourself an official reprimand. If you say a curse word that could have sexual or sexist implications, you might receive a significantly more serious punishment. As long as you are the new kid on the block, avoid using language that will make your employer wonder if he or she made the right choice by hiring you.

MISTAKE 24
Yelling...

You might be thinking, *"OK, I can raise my voice without cursing. Then the students will know I mean business without me getting myself in trouble."*

You could use this approach, but I think you will find students do not respond well when adults lose their composure. Screaming and yelling does not convey control of your classroom. In fact, your students might lose respect for you once they learn they can get you riled up and off track from teaching. Some of them might even try to make you upset on purpose just because they know it is possible.

Furthermore, you risk falling into clichés that will only aggravate and frustrate you more. Yelling might earn a female teacher the label of an "irrational woman" or a male teacher "angry man." It simply is not a measure that will win you respect in any situation.

Keeping your composure in the classroom is about more than just maintaining professionalism or not giving administration a reason to question your qualifications to do your job. Remaining calm and restoring order in your classroom, even when things start to get out of hand, is about making sure the students know you are always in the lead. When you calmly handle a mounting situation without letting it rile you, students can see that you are in control of the classroom, and they will respond accordingly.

One of the most important ways you can keep control of your classroom, without getting to the point of losing your cool and yelling at your students, is to not let little things mount up. When you ignore small issues of misbehavior or let little things slide, some students will continue to test you to see how far they can push you before you respond and do something. If you address misdeeds early on with increasing forms of discipline as the offense increases, you can let your students know you mean business without reaching a level of frustration that will lead to yelling and screaming. So be sure to address issues early and not let them build up. This should help you remain calm and professional even as students test the limits of your patience.

MISTAKE 25

Getting physical...

This point likely goes without saying. You are teaching adults, and when one adult gets physical with another, the results can ultimately involve a police report. Not only would it be the highest level of unprofessionalism to physically harm a student, it could result in a lawsuit, firing, or more serious negative repercussions for you.

With that said, there might be times when you need to remove a student from your classroom for the safety of your other students or for your own productivity. If you need to force a student to leave, do so with as little contact as possible. You can always dismiss the class or call security and let them handle the student if the conflict becomes that severe.

MISTAKE 26

Locking students in/out...

Some professors have a very strict tardy policy while others are more lax about students walking in and out of their class. If you want to have a strict policy about bathroom breaks, tardiness, and leaving early – be sure to communicate those standards in your syllabus and on the first day of class. That way all – or at least most – of your students know and understand your rules.

However, no matter what your policy is regarding late arrivals or early departures, do not lock your classroom doors. On more than one occasion, I have heard of professors who would lock their doors at the start of class or testing. While this practice does enforce your rule, it creates a dangerous situation that could make you liable in the case of an emergency.

At any given point in time, an emergency such as a fire, campus disturbance, weather conditions, or security issues can arise and your students could need to evacuate the room quickly. Also, if electronic communications break down, someone may need to get into your classroom to make you aware of an emergency or security issue. Locking the doors prevents both of these scenarios from taking place. Should anyone be hurt as a result of your actions, you could be sued, fired, or even face criminal charges. The risks far outweighs the reward in this situation.

Punishment that Might Create Resentment

While I have and will continue to emphasize that trying to be your students' best friend will not help you maintain control of your classroom, there are some discipline measures that will create unnecessary resentment. The "mistakes" I detail in this section may – at times – seem like a good idea. Just make note of the possible downsides and if you decide to employ these strategies, and be aware of the potential results.

MISTAKE 27
Using group punishment...

Surprisingly, I have heard that if a class starts to get out of hand, an instructor might punish the students as a group. I do not know if this is done because the professor cannot tell where the source of the disruption lies or because they are just frustrated with the group. But adopting this policy (such as ending a test early for the entire group because you keep hearing noises) creates a "you" against "them" dynamic in the classroom. While you do not necessarily need every student to love you, it should not be your goal to be seen as their adversary either. When you create this dichotomy in your classroom, it will become more difficult for you to reach out to students who need help and to reward students for their achievements.

Finally, in the group punishment scenario, students will recognize that you are unable to get the few students under control who are causing the disruption. This will consciously or unconsciously lead to the students to lose respect for you. Furthermore, if the students believe they will be punished anyway, rather than continue to behave well, they might decide to join in the bad behavior of the initiators.

MISTAKE 28
Assigning extra work as punishment...

While there might be a time and place to use this strategy, generally speaking, I believe that giving extra work to the class for negative behavior of a few – or even several students – is a mistake. First, both class work and homework should be thought of as a tool for learning. Teaching your students that their work has another purpose – a negative one at that –

could undermine what you are trying to accomplish by attempting to teach them learning is fun.

Additionally, your students likely have a fair amount of work to get through without extra work. Assigning this type of punishment could adversely impact a student's ability to complete their assignments and get good grades. The last thing you want to do is make it harder for your students to excel in your classroom. Doing so will cause many of your students to stop caring and putting in their full effort.

Finally, the extra work punishment – particularly when assigned to the entire class – has all of the downsides of the group punishment mistake. You will do more to earn your students' respect if you show them you can deal with disruptive students and minor interruptions without punishing the innocent in the process.

The one exception to this policy is not really a matter of when and if you should assign "extra" work, but if the class has been derailed enough – the class work might need to become homework. Your students are less likely to see this as a punishment and more as a result of the classroom disruptions. While they might believe you should get the rowdy students in line so they do not have to do their work at home, they will understand that they are not being asked to do anything above and beyond what you already had planned for them.

MISTAKE 29

Forgetting to reward good behavior...

While you need to have a discipline plan in place and be prepared to use it to maintain control of your classroom, do not forget that one of the best ways to encourage good behavior is to recognize it, point it out to the class, and reward it.

You need to take care to not call any one student out too much in order to avoid the appearance of favoritism. All of your students will most likely exhibit good behavior at one time or another. Even your most disruptive student will do something worthy of praise, if you look for it. Take those moments to reward or praise good behavior and reinforce the idea that they can receive attention for being good – not just being a clown.

Try to remember that teens are disruptive for a whole host of reasons. You do not necessarily need to identify the motivating factor behind a student's misbehavior, but do remember to use the "carrot" along with the "stick." When you praise a student who normally gets noticed for acting out, you might see them try to earn your attention for those positive actions instead of negative actions. If successful, this tactic could go as far as turning around their school performance due to your classroom management.

PART
TWO

CURRICULUM DEVELOPMENT & DELIVERY

You studied for years to earn your teaching degree and probably even worked to be certified in specific subject areas. You know your material well and are excited about teaching it to your students. If only teaching was as simple as that, because it is not. When teaching your material, there are many mistakes you can make, and there are an even greater number of errors you can make when testing or evaluating your students on what they have learned. This section is dedicated to reviewing the obstacles you should avoid in regards to teaching, homework, testing, grading, and so on.

CHAPTER 5
Planning & Preparation

Have you ever heard the saying, "An ounce of preparation is worth a pound of cure"? It is, of course, a common expression that promotes the merits of planning ahead; age-old expressions have so much basic truth to them. This one was quoted by Benjamin Franklin and might be one of the most essential truths any teacher could follow.

As a new teacher, you will report "for duty" well before the first day of school. You will have meetings, planning sessions, and even more meetings on top of that to learn about standard operating procedures, policy changes handed down by the institution, and general goals set by your department heads. This process is important for you to familiarize yourself with your new school and get comfortable in your new role.

While you attend these meetings, getting to know your fellow faculty, and counting down the days until your students arrive, your classroom and curriculum planning needs to already have begun. No matter what grade level or subject you are teaching, you will have to select curriculum, plan the course, create a syllabus, and begin making lecture notes well before your first day of class. Read on for mistakes you want to avoid in the planning process that could sabotage your success before your classes even get started.

MISTAKE 30

Selecting required reading that is costly...

Even in your first year, you will most likely have the privilege – or responsibility – of selecting the required reading material for your course(s). Whether or not you are a recent graduate or someone who worked in the corporate world prior to returning to academia, you can likely remember how expensive college books were and how happy you were when you could find used copies of your textbooks.

If you have forgotten how costly an endeavor purchasing textbooks can be, I recommend that you visit your campus bookstore and price out what it would cost to procure books for a full-load of classes in a single semester. Now that you have re-familiarized yourself with the high price of college textbooks, try to keep that in mind when you select the required reading material for your class.

When selecting your textbooks, if you can use a book and edition that has been in use at your university for at least a year, you will give your students the opportunity to purchase "used" books. If you must select textbooks that will be new to the school, try to choose ones that are cost efficient.

MISTAKE 31

Selecting required reading that is too hard to find...

As a continuation of the previous concept, when you select additional reading material, articles, and textbooks, try to make sure you can put copies on hold for check-out at your campus library. If possible, put several copies on hold so that multiple students can check out the material simultaneously.

If you want to reference several articles throughout your course, consider having them copied, bound and made available for purchase through a local bookstore. This might add some cost for your students, but it could make their ability to access important articles easier than going to the library to look them up and copy them.

MISTAKE 32

Not planning out your lectures and tests for the semester...

When building your curriculum plan for the year, you should go ahead and try to block out the material you will cover each week and when you will assign major papers, projects, or tests. The university may schedule your finals exam week for you, but beyond that, identifying dates for tests and project deadlines will be your job. Doing so ahead of time and putting those dates on your syllabus will help your students structure and plan their entire semester. While you could insist that it is not your job to help your students with their other classes, providing them an outline to schedule with will help them give their best effort not just to other classes, but to yours as well.

It is understandable that you will not be able to properly anticipate how each lecture will go and how long it will take you to cover each subject matter. As a result, you might need to move smaller assignments such as quizzes or labs/experiments. The more you teach, the more you will be able to accurately predict where these assignments will fall in your schedule, but it is unnecessary to detail every aspect of the course in your syllabus.

However, plan the big things and communicate them on the syllabus. "Give them test days the first day of class and stick with them," says Shannon Bow O'Brien, from the University of Texas, Austin. "Move material off tests if you have to, but respect the fact students may have requested days off work, scheduled babysitters, or setup their personal schedules based on your test days. If you move the test, you will cause yourself headaches," she explained.

By providing your students a general overview with a footnote that due dates and test dates are subject to change (under only the most dire set of circumstances), you have provided a calendar for them to plan around in terms of other course work, requesting time off part-time jobs, and even travel between home and school.

MISTAKE 33

Not communicating a curriculum plan in your syllabus...

By planning out your semester, you give yourself an outline to follow and can provide your students with a guideline as well. However, you need to communicate your curriculum plan and required reading on your syllabus. That way, your students have a plan in writing that they can follow the entire semester. Being detailed in your syllabus communications should lessen the amount of students that come to you later with issues or surprises. I wish I could say it would eliminate such problems, but some students will lose their syllabus five minutes after they walk out of your classroom.

Therefore, you should also upload your syllabus to your webpage and provide frequent updates to your classroom schedule so that your site becomes a resource for students as changes come up throughout the semester. If you need to cancel a class or push back a major assignment, putting notes on your webpage is a great way to communicate with your students.

You should also include your grading policies, academic policies, classroom rules, and pretty much any other important facts from your syllabus on your webpage. That way, if your students lose their paper syllabus, they can use your webpage as a constant resource.

Finally, make sure to connect your email to your webpage so students can contact you directly from your website and you are able to respond to student inquiries quickly.

MISTAKE 34
Not detailing your academic/grading policies in the syllabus…

At some schools – particularly private institutions – your entire department might have a set grading scale, defined policies for testing, or specific procedures for accepting late assignments. However, in most cases, you are going to determine your own grading scale, what percentage of the grade will depend on tests, homework, etc…, and all other aspects of how subject mastery will be measured in your class.

You will need to define all of this before your class begins so you can communicate it in detail in your syllabus. In order to avoid any accusations of favoritism or inconsistencies later, you need to set and communicate your grading policies at the start of the semester so that students know what to expect. If you need help brainstorming this issue, consider the following:

Define your grading scale: Many professors use a simple 10-point scale to break down grades with 90 and above being an A, 80-89 being a B, etc. This is what most students probably encountered in high school and what they will grasp best, so it is highly recommended. However, if you use a different scale, make sure to communicate properly to the students at the start of the semester so there are no surprises when a 92 equates to a B instead of an A. You will also need to decide if you are going to allow for plus grades (B+, C+) and what those numeric cutoffs will be. If your institution does not provide weight for plus grades in terms of GPA, it might not be necessary for you to even include them. Consult your colleagues about their policies if you are unsure what to do in this situation.

Let students know if you grade on a curve or if competitive grading will be involved in determining their final grades: If students know ahead of time that you will only assign 10 percent of the class As, they might elect to drop your class. Students should know ahead of time if they will be measured against their classmates. If you do not communicate this fully, you could face serious complaints and questions from your administration.

Tell students how their grades will be measured: Once you decide how you will measure mastery of your curriculum (tests, homework, papers, presentations, labs, etc...), you need to decide how much any aspect is going to represent a student's final grade. If you plan to average three test scores together to determine 50 percent of the students' grades, you need to outline that in the syllabus. If a research paper will represent 25 percent of the final grade, that needs to be communicated as well. If you want to allow yourself some flexibility to enhance the grade of students who attend each class but do not do as well on tests, add in a 10 percent attendance/class participation grade. Just make sure your students know and understand how their grades will be determined so you can reference it later if they claim they did not know something would be so important.

Communicate policies regarding late assignments: If you plan to deduct points when a student turns in a paper or assignment late, that should be detailed in your syllabus and reiterated later when providing instructions for the assignment.

No matter what your grading rules/policies are for your classroom, making sure your students know what to expect early on in the semester is important. That way, there is no confusion as time passes and grades are released.

MISTAKE 35

Not providing students with office hours and contact information...

While you might not be sure when you want to see students, you need to define office hours before the semester starts, communicate them on your syllabus (and website), and maintain them throughout the year. It is very important that your students feel like they have access to you outside of the classroom. And it is important for you to be able to address individual student concerns outside of your classroom so that your lecture does not get derailed too frequently.

I advise that you try to either arrive at your class a little early or be prepared to stay a little after to address student question and concerns. However, you might face scheduling conflicts with the space and need to encourage students to visit your office. If you have any say in your teaching schedule, try to give yourself time between classes to talk with students. But if all else fails, make certain that you can turn to a student and say, "I have to be somewhere in a few minutes, but if you can come by my office tomorrow, we can discuss this issue more then."

In addition to scheduling and keeping office hours, you also need to provide your students with contact information that includes an office phone number and university email. You might also want to consider providing students with a cell phone number (but not your home number) if you are not frequently in your office. For example, an adjunct professor might not maintain as much of a presence on campus as a full-time associate professor. Therefore, you might want to allow students to access you via cell phone.

You need to maintain a certain amount of privacy in regards to your students while allowing them solid lines of communication. For example, if you use a lot of social media, you might want to consider leveraging Twitter to provide your students with updates regarding your class or curriculum. However, I would advise against connecting with your students on Facebook as that might be too close to fraternizing.

Of course, how much personal contact you have with your students might depend on whether or not you are teaching undergraduates, graduate students, or PhD candidates. The higher level degree your students are pursuing, the greater the possibility they will eventually transition from being your student to being your colleague. If you are somewhat unsure how to handle your more advanced students, follow the lead of other professors in your department, but err on the side of maintaining professionalism. You can always relax your standards a bit more as you get more accustomed to your work environment.

MISTAKE 36

Not anticipating extra students in your class ...

Last-minute registrations are a given. Even if your class is full, students might change their schedules around at the last minute to accommodate a different class or help them meet a graduation requirement. For whatever reason, your class roster may not be the same when school begins as when you first showed up to work. As a result, you should be prepared to add or lose students that first week of school.

This means you should make a few extras of whatever handouts or work you are going to disperse. Make adjustments to seating arrangements (if you had one), be prepared to request additional classroom resources if you need them, and even help students who might not have been able to buy required course materials because things are on back-order. Basically, be comfortable with the fact that your best laid plans might be at least partially swept aside for late additions or changes to your student body.

MISTAKE 37

Not emailing your students before the semester begins...

The best thing you can do to start off your semester is to send your students an email before the semester even begins. There are several things you can gain by doing this:

- You can send them the syllabus in advance, giving them a chance to read it through.

- You can give them their first assignment ahead of time, which gives them plenty of time to come prepared.

- You can make sure they have the correct book titles and editions, which ensures that they come to class the first day with the correct material.

- You can introduce yourself and encourage your students to introduce themselves to you.

- You can ask them to complete an assignment for the first day of class, not only preparing them for the hard work ahead, but allowing you to set your challenging standards ahead of time.

- You can ensure that they are indeed enrolled in the correct class.

Introducing your students to your class through a pre-semester email is a great way to start your semester fully prepared.

Not only do you leave a great impression of yourself as an excellent teacher, but if any problems do come up concerning enrollment issues or an out-of-stock book, you can resolve the problem before school begins. Nothing is worse than losing valuable class time the first week of school.

CHAPTER 6
Fairness & Consistency

Whew! You made it through your first day/week of school – it should be all downhill from here. OK, not really. Putting student faces with the names on your roster was the easy part, now the work begins. The first thing you must realize is that you are teaching young adults who are on the cusp of real responsibility. Many of your 18 to 22-year-olds are not fully-fledged adults yet.

Of course, this does not apply to all of your students. Depending on your institution, you might be teaching older students, married foreign-exchange students, and students who are taking a non-traditional route though college. But chances are great that you will deal with personalities that can still be highly formed, and you will still influence these students in such as way that impacts the rest of their lives.

You must accept that they are largely who they are going to be without forgetting that you can still have a strong impact on their learning experience and desire to learn. Your best and worst moments may very well be remembered for decades to come, even when your students are grown and working in a wide-range of professional fields.

Understanding that you are important to these students without presuming that you can really alter their natural personalities is a vital step in ensuring your success as a teacher. At some point in time, you probably took a Myers-Briggs personality test and can tell if you are an ESTJ or an IIFP or one of the other 14 personality types this test identifies.

However, you might be surprised to learn that there are dozens of personality tests that can even be administered for children. From tests that will code a person as a lion, beaver, otter, or golden retriever to those that will tell you if a student is choleric, sanguine, melancholy, or phlegmatic. I am not advocating one particular coding system over another or suggesting that you give your students personality tests. I am simply reminding you that much of a person's personality is determined from birth.

Therefore, the student in your classroom that is extremely talkative is probably not trying to drive you crazy but is that way because that is how they process information. Another student who gets upset when stories do not have a happy ending or when you discuss tragedies such as the attacks on 9/11 might not be emotionally unstable, but is just a highly sensitive individual.

Throughout your teaching career, you will encounter personalities in students that gel well with your own and are easy for you to teach, as well as ones that grate on your nerves in a way you never would have thought possible. You must learn to manage and work with diverse personalities as a teacher because you will likely encounter them all.

Try to remember that diversity is the spice of life, and managing all of these personalities is one of the key leadership skills that will mark your success as a teacher. In fact, at several points in this book, I will emphasize and discuss the differences between students that can span personality, race, culture, gender, puberty, and so much more. However, though all of your students are unique, you need to ensure there is no perception that you are favoring or discriminating against any subset of students. This chapter emphasizes how fair and consistent treatment will benefit you in classroom management.

Student Equality

In a later portion of this book, I will dedicate a considerable amount of space to the relationships you form with your students and if you want to be perceived as a hard/strict teacher or a pushover. However, I cannot in good faith discuss discipline in the classroom without going over some basic classroom management strategies for maintaining control over your classroom.

You probably already realize you will have problem students, which can range from a disrespectful student to the "class clown." Dealing with students who disrupt your lessons may be more difficult than teaching the material itself. You must manage outbursts with professionalism while taking steps to minimize how often these interruptions occur.

What you might not realize is that it is not just the "bad" students who can sidetrack your lesson; very good, curious students can do it as well. While I was too quiet and shy in school to be this child, I am most certainly the mother of two such students. Either of my children could charm the heck out of a teacher while taking over their class – without really even meaning to.

When an individual is naturally curious about a concept or lesson you are teaching, it is easy to get caught up in that teaching moment. After all, this is your dream! A student is engaged and really interested in what you are teaching them, they are asking challenging questions and seem genuinely interested in the answers. And frankly, you need to be able to leave your lesson plan behind for a moment or two when the class shows an interest in something and gives you an opportunity to go into greater depth.

However, as tempting as it would be to go off on a learning tangent every time the opportunity arises, you have to keep your lesson plans more or less on track. And if you deviate from those plans, it needs to be at your discretion when you feel it would benefit the majority of your students. The following are recommendations on how to keep control of your classroom when students become disruptive for any reason:

MISTAKE 38
Letting your smartest students direct the class...

Gifted or advanced students can run the gamut in their personalities; some will be shy and quiet while others will be very outgoing and talkative. Every now and then, you will run into one who is charming and curious and will be able to all too easily dictate how the class goes if you let them.

Assuming they are not rude little "know-it-alls" who think they know more than you do, you will probably enjoy these students in your classroom. You will enjoy the questions they ask and knowing that if you call on them, they will likely have the answer, or at least something interesting to say. These students will likely make straight A's – or close to it – and will make you look good on tests and evaluations that could impact your job.

However, it is for the benefit of the entire class, that you not allow these students to become "teacher's pets." You do not want to appear to favor these students over others because that will hurt your ability to engage your entire class. Furthermore, while many advanced students find it easy to interact with adults, they still need to be able to function well among their peers. Being perceived as a "favorite" with the teacher may not benefit them with the other students.

On the other hand, you do not want to stifle these students or their desire to learn. Therefore, find ways to manage their participation in your classroom. Schedule group discussion sessions where all of your students can talk out an issue and learn from each other. Or orchestrate "teams" where you break up your most outgoing students and ask questions that will earn the groups extra credit. This will help the most ostentatious students at least earn some popularity with their peers rather than resentment.

If you are lecturing or doing a presentation, tell the students to take notes and write questions on a note card or piece of paper. Then at the end of your presentation, collect the papers in a box and pull out five to discuss as a class. You can bypass any card or paper left blank and just address the questions you find. Once you complete this discussion period, tell the students that can ask you additional questions after class.

Employing these strategies allows you to control the pace and direction of your class while still engaging your more advanced students. Additionally, it protects them from gaining a "know-it-all" reputation among their peers that is not always well-received.

MISTAKE 39
Letting "big" personalities overshadow you...

In the previous scenario, the "gifted" student might have a big personality, but they are not the only individual who can overshadow you in the classroom. From the overly disruptive student to the "class clown" there are several "big" personalities that can seize control of your classroom if you let them. You need to identify early who these students are and make sure you have strategies in mind on how to manage these students so you do not find yourself trying to wrestle control back from them later in the school year.

Young adults seek attention in many ways for a wide variety of reasons and all too often, older adults overlook bad behavior believing that the student in question just needs a little attention and everything will be fine. It would be nice to think that any student that is "acting up" in your classroom just needs a little positive attention and reinforcement, and if you give it to them all will be well. However, that is not always the case.

It might not be your attention the student is seeking at all. It could be the attention of their parents, the focus of a girl or boy they like, or just popularity among their peers. Some students might believe that if they can make the class laugh, everyone will like them. Or, they could be using "clowning around" as a cover for hiding a learning deficiency, the inability to read, or other things that make them feel inadequate.

You want to make sure that you pay attention to the reasons why the student is behaving in the manner they are and ensure that you use the proper discipline measures to not lose control of your classroom. A disruptive student might need to sit by him or herself for a while, or be sent out of the room. A student who is clowning around might need to be separated from his or her audience. If the class is not functioning well in the midst of one activity, you might need to change activities to calm your students down.

MISTAKE 40
Glossing over "easy" material...

Do not be tempted to gloss over material that you think is easy. Chances are there is at least one student in the classroom who cannot keep up. You want to give everyone a fighting chance at a great education, so instead of glossing over the easier material, give a short introduction or recap.

You can always ask the class if they know what "X" is or what "X" means, but this will not always work. If no one raises his or her hand, that one student who is confused will not want to be singled out as the only one who does not understand. Because of this, you need to be conscious of your students.

Try to analyze their behavior — do they look confused? When they turn in work, consider bringing them into your office to discuss an area that you feel they do not understand. This will help your students to avoid any humiliation in the classroom, and it will allow you to respect all levels of ability.

MISTAKE 41

Being too hard on students who ask too many questions…

While it is important to maintain control of your classroom, you should be careful on how you deal with students who are too talkative, particularly those who want to talk about academic subjects. If a student is whispering to a friend about their favorite television show or their dating life, that is the kind of talking you absolutely should silence.

However, if a student is talking about school subjects and asking questions, you need to carefully instruct them to be quiet and tell them you will go over some of their questions later. Many students are far too shy to answer a teacher's questions in class. Others are quick to raise their hands and always want to show how smart they are. You need to make sure you can engage the reluctant participants without stifling the natural participatory instincts of those who are willing to speak out.

Imagine that you have a naturally curious student who enjoys answering or asking questions and feels no awkwardness when it comes time for class discussion. However, if you are critical of this student – particularly in front of the class – you will gradually create a scenario where he or she does so less and less as the year goes on. By the end of the semester, you notice the student is not raising his or her hand anymore and has gone from being gregarious to quiet.

The lesson has stuck. The once vibrant, excited learner has become a student who is quiet and not likely to volunteer in class. He or she will meekly give answers when called upon by future teachers and will continue to get good grades, but some enthusiasm for learning has been squelched. Would you want to be the teacher who made that impact?

Instead of forever being remembered as the teacher who made Jim or Janet not want to participate in class, you have the opportunity to teach the young man or woman about situational timing – that there is a time and place for certain kinds of behavior and that he or she needs to be patient and wait until the right moment to talk and ask questions.

If you have a student that is distracting you from progressing through a lesson by asking a lot of questions, try designating a question and answer or discussion period at the end of the lesson. Have your students write down their questions as they think of them and then they can ask any that you might not have covered once the lecture is finished. This will allow the "talkative" student a chance to ask their questions in an appropriate format while also learning about adhering to the structure of a classroom.

Avoiding Inconsistencies

One of the most common pieces of advice parenting magazines offer is that children need consistency. While randomness is a fact of life, as many of your students will only be transitioning into adulthood, it might not be a bad idea to pay attention to some of the more common recommendations for parents and adopt them into your classroom. As clichéd as this principle may seem, being consistent in your classroom will serve you well.

If you allow yourself to be inconsistent in how you treat your students, you could alienate some of them without even realizing it. You know that even though all students are equal, they are not the same – some of them will be brighter than others, some of them will be more athletically gifted, others will be more attractive, and some will just possess an air of likability. If you are being honest with yourself, you will like some of your students better than others. However, you can never let that show.

You must make your students believe that only you care about one thing – educating all of them to the best of your ability.

Along with avoiding inconsistencies in how you treat one student from another, you should avoid irregularity in how you manage your classroom. Certainly, there are many things in your personal life that can impact your work. It is acceptable to have some minor deviations in your day-to-day teaching efforts based on whether or not you are having a bad day or woke up feeling monumentally inspired with just the right idea on how to communicate a concept to your students. It is, however, a poor teacher who behaves erratically from week to week, enforcing rules one time while letting things slide another.

If you want your students to respect you, follow your rules, and demonstrate their best behavior; you need to condition them on what to expect. If you are unpredictable and they are left guessing as to what the consequence of an action will be, they might be unable to decide if the action is one they wish to make or bypass. Being consistent in how you handle the same situation with every student will help your students understand that you mean what you say and that you are to be respected. The following mistakes are ones you should avoid, even if you do not currently understand why. Consider the advice below:

MISTAKE 42

Being relaxed one day and firm the next...

The way you manage your classroom during the year is the way your students will expect you to manage it all year long. If you begin in a relaxed manner, it will be difficult to become stricter later in the year if you do not have as much control

MISTAKE 42

over your classroom as you might like. If you joke and laugh with the students about poor behavior one day, the co-eds in your class will expect you to always overlook such conduct. Letting small violations pass will only confuse students later if you try to enforce harder standards.

Furthermore, if you are strict for several days, lighten up, then become strict again, you will utterly confound the students in your classroom. You will leave them lacking the understanding of how to behave and what to expect from you. While your change in teaching style and/or mood could be completely independent of the students and simply a product of your personal life, you will still leave the students wondering if they are somehow causing the changes you are demonstrating.

In the worst possible scenario, your shifting mood and teaching style could damage your ability to teach effectively. If you want to protect your ability to positively impact your students and communicate your lesson plan, you will want to minimize anything that could distract from the education process. Among many other things that could have a negative impact, your inconsistent behavior is at the top of the list. When students are left wondering how the teacher will act from one week to the next, they are not fully focused on learning. You will want to limit how often this occurs.

MISTAKE 43

Showing favoritism...

As I have previously mentioned, you can go ahead and draw the conclusion that you will have favorite students. While a parent might be able to hold off from favoring one child over another if they have a few children, in a classroom with 25 students or more, it is very likely you will have a few students who you like better than others. You might even have a student or two that you look at and think, *"My job would be so much easier if they were all like him (her)."*

There is nothing wrong with feeling that way inside. The mistake you must avoid is showing your feelings of favoritism to the student and/or class. There are many reasons you should avoid favoritism, besides the clear lack of professionalism it denotes. This favor from you could turn into claims of racism or sexism if a parent decides to bring it to your principal's attention. So, the first reason to avoid favoritism is that it could be used against you in a complaint.

The greater the possibility that such a complaint could get out of hand – *Ms. Smith does not like black students; Mr. Jones does not treat women the same as men* – only worsens the professional hit you might take. Please remember that while most people realize that students (and even their parents if they get involved) are capable of complaining for no reason — you are a new teacher. Your boss does not know you as well as a seasoned veteran and chances are, that if a formal complaint is filed, he or she might think twice before they risk their own career to vouch for you. It is best to be cautious early in your career and avoid mistakes that could lead people to forming negative opinions of you.

Showing favoritism could also limit your teaching impact on your entire classroom. First, you could create over-confidence in the students you favor, enabling them to believe that they are "better than" or "more deserving" than their counterparts. Second, demonstrating favor to your students could lead some of them to conclude that you do not care if they master the material just as long as your "favorites" do. Always calling on one or two students because you know they know the answer could lead some students to stop trying to answer questions or make them feel too embarrassed to volunteer. You must strike a balance between rewarding those students who perform well and propping up the students in your classroom who need extra assistance.

MISTAKE 44
Showing dislike for a student...

On the flip side of the same coin of favoritism is showing disdain for any one student or group of students. The first thing you should probably ask yourself is, if you do have any preconceived ideas about people based on race, gender, and religion. You should ask yourself if you are prepared to teach students of all races, religions, and even sexual orientations.

Depending on the size of your institution or the area of the country you live in, the diversity issues you will encounter in your classroom could vary significantly. But the chance that you will teach minorities of any and all kinds certainly exists. You will encounter students with diverse belief systems, cultural norms, and gender identities, and you will need to maintain a level of professionalism in your classroom (protecting these students from bullying and harassment), while not communicating any negative, private thoughts you might have about the individual students.

The above scenarios might be the most extreme, but they are certainly worth considering. A likely possibility is that you will have teens or young adults in your classroom that you simply dislike. Perhaps one of your students is a bit of a "mean girl" and she brings back memories of mistreatment you experienced yourself at that age. You could have a student who never turns in homework, does poorly on tests, and just does not seem to care about anything you are trying to teach.

Regardless of how much you dislike a student, do not show it – not to the student or the class. The first thing you should keep in mind is that even if you do not reach that student in the first month or several weeks of school, you could still make an impact by the end of the semester. Do not rob yourself of the victory of teaching a student who others would give up on – particularly if this student is unsure if they belong in college or not. You must also hold the most difficult, problematic student in your classroom as an example to all the others. If you care about that individual, then you care about them all. This is a message that your students will pick up on and internalize whether you realize it or not.

Do not be harder on some students and easier on others. If you operate your classroom in a consistent manner, students will be less likely to pick up on who is your favorite student and which one is your worst nightmare.

MISTAKE 45

Letting one student do everything on "group" assignments...

Assigning group work or projects can be a fun way for students to interact and learn – not just about the material, but from each other. Students come from a wide-range of backgrounds with vastly different life experiences. While that might not matter in a science or math lab, learning each other's perspective can open new doors of understanding in a psychology or political science course. Group work tends to facilitate this learning experience quite well.

However, this experience tends to lend itself to one or two students doing all the work. Some students are natural leaders or so concerned about their grades that they want to take control of the work. These students will naturally enable more relaxed students to not put in their fair share of effort. In early grades, this dynamic might not be so bad. However, as students get older, one of the most common criticisms of advanced students is that they always end up doing all the work on group projects.

The tendency for smarter students to willingly do all the work, while other students goof off, could have something to do with the tendency for gifted students to be introverts. According to studies, about 60 percent of gifted children are introverted compared with 30 percent of the general population. Furthermore, approximately 75 percent of highly gifted children are introverted (Silverman 2014).

While there are certainly advanced students who are extroverts, it is far more likely that you will find introverts among your gifted children. This means that while they are perfectly capable of carrying the load of a group assignment, they do not have the natural leadership and people-management skills to make sure all members of the group contribute to the work.

Instead, gifted students will do the work for the group while resenting other members who are goofing off and having fun. After several years of doing this, these students will care enough about their grades in college to just assume the role or work – hardly without even asking their classmates for ideas or contributions. This limits the learning experience for all students.

That is not to say that I think you should strike group work off your teaching methodology – though I am certain some introverts would be happy if I did recommend just that. Instead, monitor your group work. Walk around the classroom and sit in on the group as they discuss ideas and complete their assignment. When they all look at you wondering if you are going to give them instruction, tell them you are only there to observe and they should proceed. Your quiet presence will ensure that for at least part of the time, all members of the group are paying attention.

As a college professor teaching nearly 50 students at a time, assigning "group" work and/or discussions might have seemed foolish, but I believed students could learn a lot from each other and that college is a place to see things from other world views. Therefore, when I assigned my students group work, I did just as I recommended above and sat in on each group.

Additionally, I asked them to "grade" each other's contributions to the group and factored those scores into their grades. Surprisingly, they tended to grade each other pretty well. I suppose they could have done this regardless of the amount of work each participant performed, but at least I provided them with an outlet to express their opinions of their teammates' work.

CHAPTER 7
Being Available to Your Students

The number of students you teach each semester will vary depending on the size of your school, the number of classes you teach, and whether you are leading large lectures, smaller discussion classes, or graduate courses. Whether you are instructing hundreds of students at any one time or merely dozens, you need to make yourself available to them.

Not all – or even most – of your students will seek you out more than once or twice in a semester, if that. However, holding office hours is a standard operating procedure for a college professor, and it happens to be beneficial to you in many ways. By encouraging open communications with your students and letting them know you are available during office hours, you can help students who need extra clarification on subject matter, inspire young co-eds who have a growing interest in your field, and mitigate any accusations that you did not take the time to address a student's learning disability or help a struggling co-ed as much as you could.

Furthermore, managing your availability to your students through office hours and tools such as email and websites, can ensure you that communications with your students does not infringe on your otherwise busy schedule. Read on for my advice about mistakes to avoid when making yourself available to your students.

MISTAKE 46
Not being available for questions before or after class...

When you are new to a teaching position, you might not get a great deal of say in the setup of your schedule. However, when possible, try to win yourself some spare time between classes where you can address student's individual concerns, answer questions about upcoming assignments, or discuss what a student might miss if they are unable to attend an upcoming class. These are questions that can easily be addressed before or after class and these small one-on-one exchanges give you an opportunity to connect names and faces and get to know your students better.

Of course, you still need to be able to end a discussion and continue on with your scheduled day. Therefore, if a student needs more than a few minutes of your time, make sure you communicate your office hours and contact information and encourage them to connect with you later. Being available to your students is important, but you cannot allow yourself to be late for your other obligations.

MISTAKE 47
Not having convenient office hours and communicating them to the students...

If you are a morning person and make it a habit of getting to your office early, you might be tempted to schedule office hours 7:30-8:30 a.m., Monday, Wednesday, and Friday. Conversely, if you are teaching a night course, you might debate scheduling your office hours right before that class.

MISTAKE 47

Try to avoid extreme scheduling like this, when students might have a hard time seeing you.

Without inconveniencing yourself, you should try to make your office hours as varied as possible. Perhaps schedule morning hours twice a week and afternoon hours twice a week. You should also be willing to schedule appointments with students during non-office hours and make sure they know that. You do not have to schedule appointments at odd times of day or night when you would not normally be on campus, but if a student needs to see you an hour later than normal, you might want to consider accommodating him or her.

MISTAKE 48

Not communicating via email or social media…

Most likely – even if you are only an adjunct professor – you will be assigned a university or college email address. No matter how many hours you are teaching, you should make sure to check your email on a regular basis. Communicating with your students via email will make your life easier as you can address a lot of questions and concerns through it so they do not need to come into your office or see you before or after class.

You also may want to consider using social media platforms such as Twitter or LinkedIn to communicate with your students. While I strongly discourage you from connecting with your students on Facebook, I do believe you can use other social media platforms in a professional enough manner that your students will benefit from your communications without the risk of over-exposure or too personal of a connection on social networking sites.

You can use Twitter to send messages regarding reading assignments, canceled classes, upcoming projects, study material for tests, and more. You also might want to make sure you collect student emails at the start of the semester so that you can send out mass email notifications when the need arises.

MISTAKE 49
Not having a web page or not using it to communicate with students…

Assembling a simple webpage that is hosted on the college or university's server is also a standard practice for professors. If you need help, the school will have technical resources at your disposal, but since a good portion of my readers grew up in the information age, chances are that you will be able to build a simple site yourself.

Your webpage should include basic information, including a photo of you and a simple biography. I would recommend putting your syllabus online along with other useful information such as instructions for papers, assignments, reminders for test dates, or review sheets for major exams.

Other material you can include would be a copy of your resume or curriculum, list of publications, or short summaries of presentations or papers you are researching.

MISTAKE 50

Not knowing if your students have special needs…

Not all "special needs" students will come with a sign that says, "I need special consideration." In fact, I can tell you from firsthand experience, one of the most frustrating experiences is learning at the end of the semester, once grades are submitted, that your student had a learning disability they were struggling with all semester. It causes you to sit there wondering why they never told you.

In any given class, there is a chance that you will have a student with ADHD, dyslexia, or difficulty seeing or hearing. If your students have learning or testing needs that you need to take into consideration, make sure you do so. Failing to comply with their special learning needs could make you subject to a lawsuit. If you can, identify students with special needs early in the year and adjust your policies and teaching strategies accordingly. Try to detail in your syllabus the importance of the student notifying you of their needs so that hopefully these situations can be dealt with early rather than later in the semester.

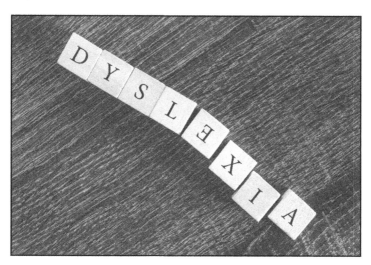

CHAPTER 8
Selecting & Structuring Curriculum

I wish I could tell you that if you can manage your classroom well then teaching will be easy as pie. I also wish I could tell you that the coursework you covered while completing your degree prepared you for every situation. The truth is that there are several challenges you will face during developing and communicating course material to your students; you might be aware of some challenges, and others could come as a surprise.

These challenges include trying to achieve the balance between creative and blended learning methodologies and not overwhelming yourself in terms of testing and grading. You could face difficulty in finding ways to engage bored students, challenge advanced students, or not get frustrated when students fail to grasp the material you are trying to teach at a fast pace.

Developing curriculum that will teach your students all the lessons they need to fulfill academic standards for their grade level might seem fairly straightforward at a first glance. However, using visual, audile, and hands-on learning techniques, while keeping yourself flexible so that you can speed up or slow down as needed, might not be very easy to do your first year of teaching.

Even though you are the teacher and prepared yourself for years to teach, you still have much to learn, and you will learn new things each year as each new group of students comes in. You have to learn about your students: what they know, what they need help in, their strengths and weaknesses, what engages and makes them love learning, and even more. In order to make the most of the school year, you must learn these things about your students early while remaining flexible as new discoveries are made throughout the year. Please review the following mistakes and see what lessons you can learn from them.

MISTAKE 51
Not doing what you do best...

"Figure out what style works for you," said Shannon Bow O'Brien. "If you are better at lecturing, then lecture. If you like small groups, use them. Do not embrace a particular teaching style because X (dissertation chair, favorite faculty member, colleague) uses it. Everyone's personality is different. For example, I HATE small group discussions in class. I hated it as a student, and I think it is a waste of time as a professor. My personal biases will always make that not work in class. I have a colleague who likes it and uses it very effectively. I do not have a problem with it because it is a style that works well for her, and she gets great results with it. However, forcing me to use it would be a disaster."

While I think it is important to mix up your teaching and testing methods, it is very important to follow Shannon's advice and not use methods that do not work well for you. If you try to push a square peg through a round hole, you and your students will suffer because of it.

MISTAKE 52
Making a grade completely dependent on test results...

There are many ways to structure a course: some classes will require lab work, others will require group or individual projects, and some will only evaluate subject mastery through a couple of tests. Some classes will require the students to write a certain number of words (referred to as Gordon rule courses in the state of Florida) over the course of the semester. Other professors will assign major research papers to include cost and benefit analysis, qualitative studies, book reviews, or statistical analysis.

Depending on the level of course you are teaching, underclassmen vs. upperclassmen or graduate level, you will be expected to assign varying degrees of complex projects or tests. My recommendation is that even for the simplest of courses, that you do not base your students' entire grades just on test scores – particularly if you use standardized question formats only.

If you teach the same course for multiple semesters, you will eventually learn what setup you prefer the most. It also might make some difference if you are teaching a short 8-week summer term vs. a full 16-week semester in the spring or fall or if your school is set up on trimesters. How much you can assign in terms of quizzes, papers, or projects will vary dramatically depending on how much time you have with students. As much as you need to diversify methods of evaluating your students, you do not want to plan assignments that will be too difficult for your students to complete or too time-consuming for you to grade.

Be sure to take all this into consideration when planning out the structure of your curriculum, including homework, tests, quizzes, essays, papers, and projects. While I do not recommend that you only use tests as your grading source, you might only have time to work in quizzes or you might be able to assign two small essays versus one large paper. Remember to structure the grading percent that your tests, quizzes, and papers represent according to the amount of work you expect each aspect to require. You do not want to under-weight or over-weight any aspects of your curriculum unless you are purposefully giving the students a method to "pad" their grades.

MISTAKE 53

Not using a diverse mix of questions on your tests...

When constructing your tests, try to keep in mind that for every student who takes one of your tests, you have to grade it. Sure, you could be fortunate enough to be assigned a teaching assistant this early in your career, but it is unlikely. Therefore, the easiest tests for you to give will be ones that can be answered on standardized test sheets and graded by your school's massive grading machines.

I could never – in good conscience – tell you not to build and assign a test that can be administered on a standard answer form, particularly if you are teaching a large lecture. However, I do believe it is a bad idea to give tests that only leverage one type of question. Whether or not you use true/false, multiple choice, or matching, I believe you need to mix and diversify your questions. Even doing this might fail to measure completely what your students have learned, but it will at least keep the tests from becoming too monotonous and hopefully keep your students' attention a little better.

When I was creating tests for my classes, I tried to blend as many different types of questions in the tests as I could. Some students actually do better at short-answer questions or essays than on true/false questions, where others do better with multiple-choice answers than fill in the blank. Using tests that include short-answers or essays might mean more work for you, but they can provide you with a better idea of what your students have learned. In order to make the grading process as simple as possible, you can use a standard test form for the majority of your questions and a blue book essay form for the hand-written portions of the test. This would still allow you the benefit of automated grading, and only require you to grade the short-answer/essay portions of the exam.

Of course, how much you need to diversify a test will depend on how many tests you give and whether or not you assign papers or essays throughout the semester. Just remember that a student who does not do well on tests might be good at making oral presentations or preparing poster boards on a special subject. If you can, incorporate these types of opportunities when teaching and evaluate how well your students are mastering the material.

Just remember that being creative and flexible in how you test, question, and grade a student will allow the majority of your class to express what they have learned and give you a better understanding of what material your students have mastered.

MISTAKE 54

Not using a mix of quizzes, papers, or essays in your grading...

As a continuation on the above section, you might not need to assign essays or short-answer questions as part of your tests, if you assign these types of grading opportunities separate from the exams themselves. Of course, this will probably still mean more grading work for you, but it breaks up the grading effort throughout the semester instead of concentrating it all at once around two or three major exams.

You can give quizzes on a regular basis that are short-essay answers and have some flexibility in how you grade them.

These regular assessments of how your students are grasping the material can also provide you with insight on what you need to cover better before you administer a major exam. On the other hand, you can simply construct some basic true/false and multiple choice quizzes that you use as a bank of test questions later. This strategy will help you when it comes time to create tests or exams and help you construct multiple versions of the same test (a strategy a lot of professors use to limit cheating).

Just remember that – as stated above – how much diversity you can use in your grading will depend greatly on the course length and setup. Do not feel like you have to use every aspect of grading – tests, homework, quizzes, papers, presentations, projects, etc..., in every course. Use a mix that works for the course you are teaching, at the level of student you have, and in the length of time you have been given.

MISTAKE 55

Not encouraging discussion in smaller classes...

If you are teaching graduate level students, discussion and debate over the material is almost expected. However, there is still room for discussion in undergraduate classes. In a very large lecture, universities might schedule discussion sections that teaching assistants will run. But at smaller schools, you can still encourage students to discuss topics if the class is small enough or break them into small groups for the same purpose.

When I had enough space to achieve it, I used to have my classes break into smaller groups and discuss some of the public policy topics we were covering in class. I would walk around the room to listen in on their discussions. In order to translate this discussion into a gradable endeavor, I would have them answer certain questions as a group. My goal of course was to expose students to other ways of thinking (I had several different demographics in my class that spanned age, race, religion, and backgrounds) while getting them to engage in the material. I cared less about their position and more about the process.

In an earlier section, I pointed out that you should not do what makes you uncomfortable, and the thought of open class discussion among your students might make you anxious. In some courses, there will be no place for it. However, if you are teaching a subject matter that would benefit from discussion or debate, try to make sure your classroom is a place that is open to it.

When studying liberal arts or social sciences, students can learn as much from each other's perspective as they can from the text or you. Additionally, creating a time and place for open discussion in your curriculum can help you manage your classroom better because you can put some questions on hold until a later point in time. This will help you cover material in the time frame allowed without discouraging discussion and debate altogether.

MISTAKE 56
Not keeping a bank of test questions saved for later use...

Some textbooks come with ready-made tests, but if you want to construct your own, you should start storing test questions in a common bank now. Assuming you will teach the same course multiple times, you can file the questions under subject or chapter headers. Not only will this make the job of creating tests easier in the future, but it will allow you to assemble multiple versions of the tests rather easily.

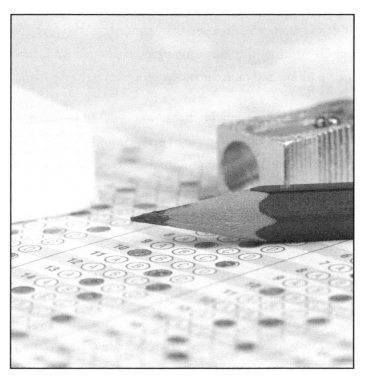

CHAPTER 9
Teaching Facts, Skills, & Concepts

When teaching at the collegiate level, you are not just teaching your students historical data and mathematical facts to memorize. You are teaching them concepts, critical thinking skills, and other skill sets they will need to carry with them into their professional lives.

Teachers communicate many facts to their students, from rules of grammar to the year Christopher Columbus came to the Americas. They help children memorize definitions, names, dates, formulas, the names of state capitals and more. These facts do not require critical thinking or analysis. Children do not need to deduct anything to regurgitate these facts on tests.

I do not mean to belittle the teaching of facts. In the time I spent teaching American Federal Government, I taught a lot of important facts to the adult students in my classroom. My tests for this course did require my students to be able to answer questions based solely on the facts and figures they memorized over the course of the class.

However, teaching is not just communication of facts; it's only a fraction of the work you do as a professor. You will need to instruct students on a diverse set of skills, including critical thinking. Facts can be memorized, but skills must be learned and then put into practice. You cannot just memorize how to read, you must practice reading to become truly proficient. Furthermore, you must be able to analyze what you have read to learn the skill of implicit reading comprehension. Helping your students learn this skill requires more than just practice. It involves discussion, debate, and engagement.

When you instruct students on concepts, you will help them not only answer the "what" question of learning, but the ever-elusive "why" question as well. I confess to being the anomaly in parenting, because I would humor the "why" question until we got to a point where I thought the explanation was beyond my child's understanding. This could be a matter of tackling a scientific concept that I was just unable to explain at the time, or it could have been that we had reached a point in a our conversation where I thought visual aids would explain the concept better than I could verbally. I do not know yet if my indulgence of the "why" game was beneficial to my children, but I believe as a teacher, you will be expected to follow in my footsteps and help students finally get their "why" answers.

Concepts teach students how things relate to one another or how processes work. Instructing students on photosynthesis is about more than teaching pure scientific facts – it involves showing students how nature ties together. When you instruct students on the parts of the flower and explain to them how pollinators move the process of pollination and help flowers reproduce, you are not just teaching facts to memorize. Students need to see how these concepts tie together in order to truly understand the subject matter.

This chapter is dedicated to the mistakes that can be made when teaching facts, skills, and concepts to students, and also to make sure your students are taking away something important from each of those categories.

MISTAKE 57

Getting frustrated with students who are not grasping the material and are not ready to move on...

Many teachers think that once a lesson is taught, it is time to move on to the next area of study. If a student or several students are lagging behind or not grasping the material, you might feel frustrated and tempted to move on and just let that material slide. While I understand that you have much ground to cover in a school year and are concerned about how the students will measure up if you lag too long in one area, it is best to be flexible with your curriculum.

If you are only losing ground with one or two students, then you can offer special tutoring to help those students catch up. But if students do not understand the lesson, then you need to take some extra time to communicate the lesson effectively. Perhaps you need to try to convey it in a new way or just spend more time working with each student one-on-one until most of your students catch on. Just remember, there might be times when your students move through material faster than you thought and things will balance out.

MISTAKE 58

Being opposed to re-teaching facts or concepts students should already know...

Students learn certain skills each year of school and they must be proficient in certain abilities to advance to the next grade. In order to gain admissions into college, it's easy to expect them to have mastered several skills. However, you might discover that all of your assumptions were wrong, which is why you should evaluate your classes early in the semester to see what your students know and what they need to learn.

After taking French for two years in high school, I decided to advance my skills in college and take a couple of semesters there as well. I can still remember my Parisian French professor looking at me after a few class sessions and saying 'Où habitez-vous?'

Required to speak only in French and not having any idea what she was saying, my only available response was "Je ne sais pas." This is, of course, my favorite French phrase and if you cannot guess what it means, it translates to "I do not know."

Now going back to the original question the professor was asking me, it translates to "Where do you live?" Did I know where I lived? Of course I did. But despite the fact that she said the phrase several times, I could not conclude what she was asking. Interestingly, when she became a little frustrated and wrote the phrase, I was able to understand it and excitedly replied "J'habite un Etats-unis!" Not a perfect turn of phrase, but it was fairly close to "I live in the United States."

My French skills have not advanced much beyond this level, and I was always able to read and write French better than I could hold a conversation. But the point of the story is that until I could see the phrase written, I was hopelessly clueless. Your students might know what you are talking about if you jog their memories a little first.

Basically, after a summer of fun and sad goodbyes (assuming you are teaching freshmen), getting your students to once again speak the same language you are using can be a challenge. So, before you decide that our education system is worse off than you ever imagined, try some board exercises or visual aids. The results might be somewhat reassuring.

However, once you get your students on the same page as you, some of them still might not remember the skills they learned years before. If they forgot, it is your job to bring their skills back up to par so you can move them toward more advanced skill sets. Therefore, any time you tackle a new subject, be prepared to review the basics before you get into the meaty part of the lesson. If you find some students in need of extensive remediation teachings, consider offering them assistance after class.

MISTAKE 59
Not reviewing after short school breaks...

You may understand the importance of reviewing material after a long summer break, but do not overlook the need to review a little after holiday breaks such as Thanksgiving, Christmas, and Spring Break. Any time a student closes their books for a week or more, there is a strong possibility they will forget the material you covered previously.

In fact, you can almost consider it a given that your students will not remember anything you covered prior to that break well enough to test on it after. Do your best to schedule section tests prior to long student breaks. If you need to administer a test after a break, spend some time reviewing the material with the students and make sure they are capable of doing well.

MISTAKE 60

Expecting every student to come into class with the same knowledge or skills...

Naturally, there are prerequisites for many courses you will teach and if your students have met those, you can expect a certain amount of subject mastery coming into the classroom. However, brace yourself to have all levels of writing ability, reading comprehension, and inaccurate preconceived notions walk through your door in entry-level courses.

More than 65 percent of high school graduates go on to attend college for some period of time. While many of them will not complete a degree, they will take several entry-level or technical courses. It is well-known that education throughout the U.S. varies in levels of quality. As a result, regardless of your institution's admissions standards, you cannot expect a standard level of knowledge and skill sets coming into your class.

If you teach at a community college, which generally has lower admissions standards, you can expect some of your students to have lower levels of certain skills sets. During my time teaching at a small university, the biggest area I found students lacking in was their writing skills. It is surprising how many college students are still making common grammatical errors or are completely incapable of spelling words correctly.

Unless you are an English professor, how much emphasis you want to place on grammar and spelling is up to you. In testing, you might not want to take off points for short answer or essay questions that contain spelling or grammatical errors. However, if you are assigning type-written papers, you should incorporate solid writing structure as part of your grading scale (at least on a minor level). If you plan to include these writings as part of your grades, be sure to include this as part of the instructions you provide the students.

In terms of courses such as sciences and math or even computer classes, just plan on covering all the basics. Do not assume you can skip over some material because your students "should have learned that in high school." Additionally, watch for students who seem to be struggling and discuss whether or not they should withdraw from your class at some point and take a lower level course if needed.

MISTAKE 61
Thinking a student is slow because they are lacking a certain skill set...

Whether or not a student is a transfer from another college, hails from a state with a bad public education system, or they just did not master a skill set they should have before coming into your classroom, you should recognize that an inability in one area does not equal a lack of ability across the board.

While most people recognize that adults are good at some things and not others, we often forget this when teaching. Even when students are being encouraged to pick majors and minors and specialize in certain fields, we can forget that even highly intelligent individuals do not necessarily excel in everything.

If your student is struggling in one skill set, do not automatically lump them in with your lower level students. Offer them extra help and encourage their improvement. You might find that once they get into other areas of the course, they are one of your top performers.

MISTAKE 62
Thinking students love your subject as much as you do...

If you are teaching upper-graduate students, the chances that they will love your subject as much as you do are much better than if you are teaching undergraduates. Even those who are majoring in your field might not enjoy your specific course as much as you love to teach it. Other times, you might be teaching students who are just taking your course because they are required to for their degree.

"The truth is that the majority of students we teach do not care about our field. They are in our classes for the credit and they will never embrace the area that same way we do. We are not trying to create clones. We are trying to express to students why we find this area interesting/important and why they should care as well. They may never love it as we do, but if we do our jobs well, they should have at least a passing respect for it," said Shannon Bow O'Brien.

If your students do not light up over the topics you are passionate about, do not be too disappointed. Lecture on and take comfort in the fact that you are teaching them something that they might be able to use later in life – even if it is not the primary focus of their future careers.

MISTAKE 63

Underestimating how hard the subject matter is to learn...

From the time you began your undergraduate journey to the time you completed your doctorate degree, you have been engaged in an elaborate effort to become an expert in your field. Your students are only at the start of this journey. Do not overestimate what they know or how difficult it will be for them to understand the material.

"Most professors, because they are specialists in their fields of study, forget how hard it was to learn material the first time," said Shannon Bow O'Brien. "It is easy to look at students and assume they are lazy or stupid. We forget how long it took for us to learn the material inside and out. We can recite long sections of material easily because we have done it for years, and we really love the field. When you see this material the first time, it often looks like a foreign language. Students struggle to make connections we take for granted. It does not mean we should give them a pass, but be more patient and understand that there is a learning curve."

CHAPTER 10
Tests & Homework

Homework and tests are an important part of your curriculum as well as quizzes, classroom participation, presentations, book reports, and various other methods you can use to evaluate if your students have mastered the material. It is important that the means you use to assess your student's understanding of the subjects you teach are properly designed for their skill level while employing several different methodologies.

Not every student will test well. Some will do better on certain types of questions (multiple choice) than others (essay). Be sure that when you design tests and homework assignments that you are not using just one method of evaluation. The most important thing to remember is that you can change your methods as the year progresses. If you try something and it does not seem to work for any of the students in your classroom, be open to altering your lesson plan accordingly. Read on for more specific discussion on both homework and testing mistakes to avoid.

MISTAKE 64

Forgetting what it is like to be a student...

The first thing to keep in mind when planning your test, homework, project, and quiz schedules is to remember what it was like to be a student. Some students will be carrying a full load of credits while others will be in school part-time while working full-time jobs and caring for families.

Again, your job is not necessarily to make things simple for your students, but you should keep in mind that you are not anyone's sole or even most important priority. When you decide how much time your students should be spending on your coursework, keep in mind the level of the course you are teaching (an entry-level course or one designed for upperclassmen) and how many students are taking your course as a general requirement vs. completing your course as part of their major.

These considerations will help you evaluate what to expect from your students and how much work you should give them. Keeping a realistic mindset about how involved your students are outside of your class will help you decide how much work to assign throughout the semester. It will also make you feel less frustrated or disappointed with the amount of effort your students are putting into your class.

MISTAKE 65

Assigning too much work...

Assigning too much work has disadvantages both for you and your students. "Many young professors often assign too much material and underestimate the amount of time it takes to grade," said Shannon Bow O'Brien. "They have very ambitious ideas about what they want to teach.

You often have to be aware of the types of students you are educating. If you teach small classes at a university where most students are single and go to school full-time, you can push those students harder than in other situations. If you teach large classes at institutions where many of your students are married, have children, or work full-time, you will need to take that into consideration as well. If your class has a large amount of material that is challenging to read in a week, then they may just skip it."

When you think about how much work you are assigning, multiply whatever you assign by about five or six times. If you are asking your students to spend three hours a week outside of class on your work and attend your class three hours a week that is a total of six hours. Multiply that by the total number of classes and you will come up with about 30 to 36 hours a week of work for students. Anything more than that and your students will not have time for part-time work, work-study, or any athletic or extracurricular pursuits. Remember your students have a lot on their plate; try not to overwhelm them.

MISTAKE 66

Not allowing more than one day to complete homework…

When it comes to helping students not get overwhelmed with homework, another bit of advice I can offer you is to give students a few days to complete all assigned homework. In high school, my Geometry teacher regularly allowed us two days to complete any assignment. We were permitted to ask questions on the day between him assigning the work and us turning it in. There was never any excuse not to get work done in his class and he was – by in large – one of the most popular teachers in the school.

I am not saying you need to always allow multiple days for homework, but you might want to consider giving students a plan at the beginning of each week regarding what they will have to complete and turn in by Friday. If they understand early how much time they need to allot for your work, they can budget their time accordingly and schedule your assignments where they can most easily complete them. Allowing your students some flexibility does not diminish their effort, but it could improve their output.

MISTAKE 67

Assigning work that your students cannot yet grasp ...

While earning my bachelors degree, I once began a course where it felt as if the professor would give us an assignment, go over the appropriate material when we all did poorly, and then give us another assignment that measured our abilities. As a result, I was ping-ponging between really poor grades and high marks. Since I did not feel comfortable talking to the professor or believe I would get the grade I needed in the course, I withdrew rather than risking a bad mark. I took the course later with a different professor and did very well.

Not all students will be as proactive as I was when they figure out that they are a bad match for a professor's teaching style. Some will trudge through the course and do poorly, earning a black mark on their transcript for no reason. If you hand out one or two assignments that score very poor grades, you should likely put some serious consideration into how you can modify your curriculum to prevent your students' failure.

I am sure you had at least one professor in college who took joy in failing students, or perhaps even more than one. He or she probably considered it a rare honor to hand out A's in the course; however, you should not consider it a mark of "toughness" if your students are having a hard time grasping the material. In fact, it is more likely a measure of your failure than your success if your students receive bad marks in your class. I am not an advocate for "grade inflation," but I do believe it should be possible for a reasonable amount of your students to achieve A's and Bs in your class.

If most of your students are floundering, look into what changes you need to make in your teaching approach. You also want to ensure your students are capable of completing an assignment before you assign it. Making yourself available for extra office hours or through email communications should help you evaluate if your students are struggling too much. You also may need to extend deadlines and adjust instructions if your students need it. Just try to apply changes or extensions to everyone when possible to avoid the appearance of favoritism.

MISTAKE 68

Not spacing out test and project due dates...

If it can be avoided, do not assign tests at the same time you have a major paper or project due. Instead, space out your assignments so students have adequate study and preparation time for each project. It can also be helpful if you schedule certain tests or quizzes on certain days of the week so that students can rely on a certain level of predictability. That will help them plan ahead.

MISTAKE 69

Assigning tests on game days or too close to holidays...

Whether you like it or not, you should pay attention to holidays and school events when assigning tests and projects. "Do not schedule tests on major game days, holidays, or the day right before or immediately after break. If your university requires a doctor's note as an excuse, all you will learn is how many of your students have friends, parents, or even a friend's parent who works in the medical fields," said Shannon Bow O'Brien.

When it comes to holidays, try to schedule tests and project due dates before breaks rather than after. Your students are more likely to study and complete work before a holiday rather than during their time off. If you scheduled homework and/or tests on a day that turns out to be bad for the students, be willing to adjust your schedule. While you cannot be completely accommodating to everything that comes up throughout the school year, you should try to give your students their best chance for success.

Fair Testing

You will always have students who believe your tests are too hard or unfair. You cannot throw out test scores or accommodate every complaint. However, you can take steps to ensure you are conducting your testing in the fairest manner possible. Make sure your tests incorporate different ways of asking questions and be willing to throw out a question if most of your students get the answer wrong. Consider the following mistakes you can avoid so that no one can falsely accuse you of being unfair in your testing.

MISTAKE 70
Only giving tests that leverage one way of learning...

The same extensive reasoning that says "teaching for tests" is a bad idea is the same reasoning that says giving tests that only use a certain type of question is a bad idea, too. Using only multiple choice or true/false types of questions that fit well with standardized tests might fail to completely measure what your students have learned.

When I was creating tests for my classes, I tried to blend as many different types of questions in the tests as I could. Some students actually do better on short-answer questions or essays than true/false, where others do better with multiple-choice answers than fill in the blank. In order to provide all of your students with a chance to excel, it makes sense to leverage multiple styles of testing/question construction.

Furthermore, some students might not do well on tests at all but are good at making oral presentations or preparing poster boards on a special subject. You need to incorporate these types of opportunities when teaching to evaluate how well your students are mastering the material.

Just remember that being creative and flexible in how you test, question, and grade a student will allow the majority of your class to express what they have learned and give you a better understanding of what material your students have mastered.

MISTAKE 71

Not using a "curve"...

I am a big believer in giving a grade that a student earns. In other words, I do not advocate passing a student who has not reached decent subject mastery just so they do not have to deal with the shame of having to retake the course. However, when I make a test, it is not a fool-proof process. When no student achieves an A on a test or very few students achieve a passing grade, there was clearly a failure in the preparation given the students or the test itself.

No teacher should feel reluctant to provide some kind of "curve" on his or her tests. My fiancé's daughter had a teacher who graded tests and then returned them to students, allowing them to open their books, correct the answers they got wrong, and receive partial credit for their corrected work. I think this is an effective way to assess what the student already knows and then allow them to learn from their mistakes.

Conversely, you can spend some time evaluating the test a bit and identify if there were questions that all (or most) the students missed. In that case, you can review the question and see if you think it was badly worded or if it was a topic you did not cover sufficiently in class. If you identify any questions like this, throw them out and re-grade the tests accordingly. Finally, you can just use a simple curve where the highest grade becomes an A or a 100, and adjust all grades from that point.

The important thing is that you realize that students talk to each other, and giving them tests where no one succeeds does not make you a "hard" teacher who demands a lot from their students. Instead, it makes you look like a bad teacher who is not doing a good job. You do not need to "go easy" on your students so you are well-liked, but you do not want them to feel like an A is out of their reach or that success is unachievable either.

I think this is an important matter for new teachers to understand because, most likely, you have just come from a collegiate environment. Since the time I completed my masters in political science at the University of Florida, I have maintained a large network of college professors. We all know that teaching methods for college professors range from "relaxed and easy" to "sadistic." If you have had one or more of those professors who starts their semester off stating proudly that they have only given three A's in 20 years, your idea of grading and "curves" might have been skewed in the process.

Try to remember that success should be within the grasp of all students. Do not be afraid to adjust your grading scale, use a curve, or provide extra credit to empower their success.

MISTAKE 72
Creating overly complex tests...

It is highly unlikely that many of your students will ever be able to understand the nuances of test questions that are looking for the most correct answer. Frankly, some of them might not be able to correctly answer any question that has more than one correct answer. Therefore, "all of the above" and "none of the above" answers might confuse them. That does not mean you cannot use those questions, just be aware that overly complex questions might fail to truly measure your students' understanding of the material.

When writing true/false questions, consider your students abilities as you decide how complex they will be. While the standard rule for true/false questions is that "If any part of the statement is false, then the entire statement is false," which is a concept that is more easily conquered by advanced students or certain kinds of analytical thinkers.

To help you decide if any question on your test is too complicated, look at how many of your students got the answer correct. If none or few of your students answered the question correctly, it might be that the question should be thrown out.

Finally, when preparing a test that will have some difficult questions to separate the A's from the Bs, be sure not to put those questions at the start of the test. "If a student has major difficulty with the first question, it affects the rest of the test," said Bill Hayes.

MISTAKE 73

Not allowing enough time for students to complete a test...

Of course you cannot allow your students to spend hours on any one test, but do make sure you are not following some "minute per question" ratio your students are not likely to meet. Be sure to either spend time explaining the test or provide detailed instructions on the test. If you are delivering the test during a normal class session, let your students know when the class is winding down so they can adjust accordingly to try to finish on time. If it seems like very few students have turned the test in when it comes time to collect the tests, you might want to take that into consideration when grading.

MISTAKE 73

When you look over the test results, if it seems like the majority of your class was unable to finish or struggled with the end of the test (in other words, they guessed), reevaluate how long you make your tests. While you cannot adjust your plans to suit every student in your classroom, you can make note of how most students are doing. If most students are doing poorly, you probably need to make things easier in some way.

MISTAKE 74

Making too many assumptions about what your students already know...

As I previously mentioned, you will have students join your class at the last minute or even later. These students may have joined you from a very different educational environment.

Students from a wide range of classroom or institution setups might mean that your students had different learning experiences and will start the semester with different knowledge and skill sets. Outside of curriculum, there are other influences that could impact what your students know and what they need to learn, ranging from contributions from their parents to extracurricular activities earlier on in their lives.

For these reasons, it is important for you to quickly assess and understand what skills, knowledge, and tools your students already possess and what they still need to master. The earlier you identify areas where your students might need extra help, the faster you can bring them up to speed and advance the whole class together.

Therefore, I recommend that you evaluate your students' abilities and knowledge the first week of classes and adjust your curriculum accordingly. This should make your whole school year run more smoothly.

CHAPTER 11
Identifying & Dealing with Cheating

Cheating is probably not an act you look forward to dealing with in your classroom, but you should definitely have a plan in mind for how to address the issue if or when it arises. If you think drawing a hard line on cheating will discourage the behavior in your classroom, you are probably correct. However, be sure that you correctly identify the student who is guilty of cheating and hand out a punishment that is appropriate for the offense.

MISTAKE 75
Punishing the wrong student for cheating...

When my daughter was in third grade, she came home one day and told me she had her spelling test taken away from her because she might have been cheating. I received no note from the teacher, and I knew my daughter would have aced the test if she had been allowed to complete it because I had reviewed the words with her all week.

I contacted the teacher and asked what happened. The teacher explained that my daughter and one of the other students were talking during the test and she had to take the tests away from students who talked based on the assumption of cheating. Thinking back, I cannot remember if this was the teacher's policy or the school's because as she explained to me, this was being done in preparation for a state-wide standardized test that was being administered at that grade level.

The students had to practice their testing as if they were taking the big standardized test later that year, which would be strictly administered to prevent cheating. Since the results of these tests can impact the funding school's receive and even a teacher's job security, I certainly understand why teachers and schools must prepare students on how to take such tests.

However, negatively impacting a good student's grades because someone speaks to them and they reply is not good policy. Fortunately, the teacher had enough flexibility to offer my daughter (and the other student) a make-up, harder version of the test. She easily made an A and learned a lesson about talking during tests.

My caution for new teachers would be to follow this example in one sense and learn from it in another. In my opinion, the only thing this teacher did wrong was she did not explain to her students what the exact punishment would be if they were caught talking during the test. She didn't tell them they would be permitted the make-up test, and she did not send home a note explaining to the parents what had happened and that there was a make-up option.

Otherwise, if you need to have a highly strict policy about talking during a test, permit a make-up option for students who are not cheating. Even if it is a harder version of the test, allowing students who engaged in a conversation that might have had nothing to do with the test itself to receive some grade is better than penalizing them with a zero. Furthermore, when one student talks, it could be to tell another person to keep their eyes on their own paper or to quiet someone who talked to them.

Assigning blame for cheating during a test or quiz is likely not a cut-and-dry issue and an innocent student can easily get caught up in your discipline measures if you are not cautious. Be sure to listen to the students. Permitting a make-up option for a first offense should not hinder your ability to keep up with your grading. If the problem persists with the same students, try rearranging the seating assignments. Also, remember that if you walk around the room while administering a test, you will automatically discourage a lot of cheating activity.

MISTAKE 76
Handling plagiarism…

Plagiarism is a very serious issue on the collegiate level and it comes in multiple forms. You could have a student who paid another person to do their work. You could have a student copy work word for word, essentially stealing the work of another person. Or your student could simply forget to use proper citation in their paper. Each possibility comes with different issues to address and the appropriate punishment varies.

First, your school likely has an honor code and a policy on student plagiarism. You should be aware of the institution's policy and communicate it thoroughly in your syllabus, as well as in the instructions you give your students prior to assigning a paper. I have even seen professors go so far as to have students sign a pledge not to plagiarize work during their writing efforts.

If you are confident your student stole work and you can prove it, you can fail them and put them up for disciplinary review. If you believe they paid for their paper to be written, you might have a harder time proving that and should probably consult a colleague before deciding what to do.

If you find that your student has merely failed to use proper citations, you should grade them accordingly but not fail their total effort.

The opportunities for students to purchase papers online is abundant. I know more than one person who earned extra money this way in college. However, this is considered cheating for both the person doing the writing and the person claiming the work as their own. If you believe your students have had a little too much help from a friend or colleague, talk to them about their effort. If during that conversation, you come to believe the student needs to put more personal work into their paper, give them the chance to write it again with a grade penalty.

Again, I realize that students have to be held accountable on the collegiate level, but providing them with the chance to complete honest work and still receive a grade (even if it comes with a penalty) will hopefully encourage them to do the work themselves in the future.

MISTAKE 77
Not creating multiple versions of a test...

One of the best ways you can avoid having students cheat is to create multiple versions of the test so that even if a student does look on their neighbors' papers, they would gain no benefit by copying their answers.

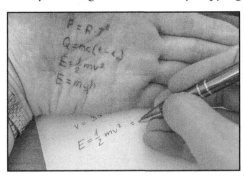

MISTAKE 78

Not having enough people present when proctoring an exam...

It is true that students can think of just about any way to cheat, maybe more than you can imagine. They are well aware that there is a risk associated with cheating, but with enough people walking around a classroom or lecture hall, they might be hesitant to try anything. Even if you do not normally have teaching assistants working for you, you should check with office staff and see if you can have help monitoring students while they take your exam if you are concerned about cheating prevention.

MISTAKE 79

Not requiring a clear workspace during testing...

No matter what age students you are teaching, there is always the possibility for distractions during testing as well as cheating. It is important that you require students to maintain a clear workspace during all testing. The environment you create in your classroom and other rules you outline for your students will determine how much energy will need to be dedicated to make this possible.

For example, if you allow drinks in your classroom, as surprising as it may seem, beverage labels can be used to jot down notes or formulas not permitted for use during testing. Therefore, it is important that you ask students to leave beverages in their backpacks or bags, or just beside them at their feet.

You should also require that all electronics are either silenced or turned off and are put away during testing. With the extreme accessibility of smartphones and small tablets that make information easier than ever to look up, you should not allow these opportunities to even arise in order to maintain a fair testing environment. With that said, the only materials that should be on students' desks during testing are writing utensils, answer recording sheets, calculators (if applicable) and the test packet itself.

CHAPTER 12
Grading

Assuming you are not one of those teachers who takes great pleasure in running a class that is impossible to pass or one who feels like they must give a certain amount of Cs and Ds to be taken seriously, you will likely want to help your students bring their grades up. Let me first say that I do not believe in handing A's out like the professors at Harvard apparently do (where recent studies show rampant grade inflation and an average grade per class of A-) (Stein 2013, Strauss 2013).

However, I do believe that any teacher can strive for their students to get as many A's or Bs as possible (without fudging their test scores to accomplish it) without considering themselves a failure for not having more students who do poorly. With that said, helping struggling students bring up their grades should be a goal of any teacher. This section is dedicated to advising first-year teachers on how to do that in an effective and efficient manner.

MISTAKE 80
Using competitive grading...

The strategy of competitive grading is one I never encountered while earning my degrees, but I do know students who had to perform in this environment. If you are unfamiliar with the concept, the idea is that only a certain percent of students will earn any specific grade. Therefore, the cut off for an A might be the top 10 percent of your students, even if 50 percent of your students might have earned what would be considered an A on most grading scales.

One concept that goes along with the idea of competitive grading is that you have to have a certain amount of students at the bottom of your scale. That would mean that even if all your students earn a passing grade on a normal grading scale, you would still "fail" some students if they were ranked in the bottom portion of your class.

I strongly recommend against use of such grading policies, as I believe that even if you communicate it with your students at the start of the semester, you could end up getting many complaints. A tenured professor who has been grading like this for decades might get away with it, but you should probably avoid the backlash it would cause.

My opinion is that if your students earn the grade – good or bad – give it to them. That means if 15 or 20 percent of your students earn an A, award them accordingly. Do not punish a good student for being in class with a lot of other good students as well.

MISTAKE 81
Not giving the student the grade they earned...

As I mentioned earlier, there is documented evidence that at elite schools, like Harvard, grade inflation has run rampant. This has been partially attributed to graduate-level teaching assistants wanting nothing to do with overly-irate students freaking out about getting a B+ instead of an A. They have their own work to complete and they just do not have time to haggle with students about a few points. As much as possible, avoid letting this seep into your grading practices (and make sure your teaching assistants are not doing it themselves).

No matter how hard a student tries, sometimes their grades will not reflect their effort. And yet, "A for Effort" should not be part of your thinking. If you have done your job throughout the school year, working to identify tests you need to curve, assignments you might need to drop because no one did well on them, providing opportunities for extra credit, etc., then you have to give your students the grades they earn.

When you are looking at the final grades, there is no telling what exactly is going to bother you. It may be a student who you know tried really hard, but still ended up with a C. It could be a student who you have to fail, in extreme cases, multiple times. Do not be tempted to "pad" grades if you feel bad for a student. You need to be able to justify those grades and show that you are being fair across the board. Whatever rules you apply to one student, you must apply to all.

MISTAKE 82
Being unwilling to fail a student...

In a previous section, I discussed in length the mistake of not using a curve when testing. However, there is a difference between curving a grade on a test or tests and padding students' grades to pass them when they would otherwise fail.

Our education system is littered with the idea that failure will hurt students, injure their self-confidence, and apparently cause insurmountable damage to their success. The pressure is so strong to pass students that many receive passing grades without learning the necessary skills to advance to higher levels. This ultimately leads to a portion of the population graduating while functionally illiterate or even worse, students who are allowed to walk on graduation day but are not receiving diplomas – just certificates of attendance. This sentiment is starting to permeate into institutions of higher learning and is something you should be aware of, since you are on the receiving end.

In the attempt to not ever make a student feel like a failure, you can often fail to give them what they need – an education. Just because you might be teaching an entire classroom of young adults who have been treated in this manner their entire lives does not mean you have to allow it to continue in your classroom. When these students graduate or leave your class, their careers will likely take ups and downs. At some point, they must learn that failure is not the worst thing that can happen to them. They need to start to understand that failure is something that can be overcome.

At most universities, there is some process for grade forgiveness. As a professor, advancing a student who is not prepared is a mistake. The plain, simple truth is sometimes you have to fail a student, but it can turn out to be the best thing for them. Failing a class and retaking it for grade forgiveness can help a student figure out whether or not they are in the wrong field of study or help them better master the subject material. Passing them on when they do not deserve it would be a disservice to their education.

MISTAKE 83
Not grading participation...

Having taught several college courses, I have structured my grading scale in numerous ways. I find that I do not like grading attendance, but I do believe it is important to grade participation. There are numerous ways to do this when teaching adults.

While some students are shy and difficult to draw out of their shells, many are open, full of questions, and more than happy to "participate" in learning activities. Engaging students in participation activities is a great way to keep their minds from wandering, prevent them from getting bored, and really help them grasp a lesson.

Since participation is a valid way to learn, you should put some grading emphasis on it. If you plan to make 10 percent of the final grade a participation grade and continue to set up activities to evaluate that grade, you are encouraging yourself not to overlook this aspect of learning.

Additionally, a student who engages in class by creating and presenting a topic through a presentation, talking about a book or study they are reading, or acting out a skit on a segment of history he or she is learning about demonstrates some subject mastery. Even if they are not able to translate that understanding of the subject into a perfect test score, they should receive some credit for their work. A minor participation grade not only helps students engage in class, but it can also bolster the confidence of a student who might not test well but is still learning.

MISTAKE 84
Not giving extra credit...

I am a big believer in extra credit. I feel if a student is on the cusp of a higher grade and they want to put in some extra work to bring it up, they should be given the opportunity to do so.

Personally, I would advise that you plan it into your tests and curriculum. Provide bonus questions on tests and assign extra credit worksheets or out-of-class assignments, such as attending relevant seminars or even dramatic performances. However, if you do not plan on giving extra credit but your students ask about it, be quick to accommodate it.

It does not take a lot of extra work to give your students an extra credit assignment, even if you plan it at the last minute. The extra grading might be a little inconvenient as the semester winds down, but not all of your students will do extra credit. So the additional work for you may not be that significant.

I have heard teachers say that "only the good students" do extra credit work or "only the students who do not need it do the extra credit." These teachers believe that practice is a waste of their time. Having taught hundreds of adults, I can assure you that the extra credit I've given has made a difference for many of my students.

A little extra work can make a difference to a student who may not have mastered the material early on. Additionally, I think working on extra credit helps students realize that a teacher does care about their grade and is willing to put in a little extra effort to help them improve.

As many of you first-year teachers can probably recall, being able to talk to your professors in college makes a difference in academic performance. Rewarding students for asking for help or extra work is a good way to develop their confidence

MISTAKE 85

Not giving all of your students the chance to do extra credit...

Of course, once you decide to allow your students the opportunity to do extra credit, you need to extend that offer to all of your students, not just those who ask for it and not just those who need it. While you might be able to identify the students it will help and those it will not make a difference for, still offer extra credit opportunities to your whole class to avoid any accusations of favoritism or unfairness.

MISTAKE 86

Not leveraging what a student excels in to help them with their weak areas...

I believe that you can help a student improve by using what they excel in to help increase their understanding and performance in areas where they are weak. For example, if you observe that the majority of your students learn well from lessons where you have incorporated visual aids, try to include them in other lessons as well. Be creative if you have to.

The reason for this recommendation is simple; everyone is good at something. Do not be afraid to use a wide-range of teaching methods to communicate your subject matter, and if something is not working, do not be afraid to change your strategy to something that works better for your classroom.

Try to remember that you designed your class material for students you did not know – for nameless, faceless students whose strengths and weaknesses you were blissfully unaware of. Now you know these students and you know what some of their interests are and what they do well, so try to customize your existing lesson plans. Be flexible and use strength to promote more strength.

MISTAKE 87

Not keeping track of grades well...

One of your most important jobs as a teacher is to evaluate your students' performance and document the results. The subsequent results must be recorded accurately and completely in order to make up students' final grades. Your school might have a method of recording grades they expect you to use, but you still need to be sure you are organized and methodical in your approach. You do not want to give back graded papers to students before you record them. Keeping track of your grades effectively will help you greatly if any student challenges your grades at the end of the year. Failing to have a good system could leave you in the lurch.

MISTAKE 88

Not frequently communicating grades to students ...

Believe it or not, there are students who anxiously await their grades or obsessively refresh their email accounts for updates after submitting a big assignment or taking an exam. Much time and effort is spent studying, and many students are eager to see if they are performing effectively. Once a student receives a less than acceptable grade, he or she may begin to evaluate whether additional action must be taken, such as asking for help or hiring a tutor. Your delay in grading tests and papers and getting that information back to students could cause more of a headache than grading said assignments in a reasonable amount of time. Make sure you are communicating well with your students and are not leaving them uninformed about your progress. If you are honest, students will be more likely to cut you some slack.

MISTAKE 89

Grading on trigger warning labeled material…

A trigger warning is supposed to signal to readers that the material that follows might be uncomfortable or upsetting. Material that has a trigger warning – literature, films, and other texts – could be labeled with the warning because it relates to sexual assault, other kinds of violence, racism, or other prejudices. Advocates of using trigger warnings on syllabuses say that students have a right to know if they will encounter sensitive material in advance (Flaherty 2014).

Assuming your university requires trigger warnings, or you decided to include them whether you needed to or not, you need to plan for complaints regardless of whether you took the necessary precautions. What do you do when one or more of your students comes to you to tell you they cannot handle the assigned material because it makes them uncomfortable?

In early 2014, student leaders at the University of California Santa Barbara presented a resolution that asked officials to adopt a mandatory trigger warning policy for class syllabi. Furthermore, they asked that professors who labeled content as "may trigger the onset of symptoms of Post-Traumatic Stress Disorder" would be required to issue advance alerts and allow students to skip those classes (Jarvie 2014).

So, if you allow students to "skip" uncomfortable lectures, reading material, and general class time because of triggers, how then do you evaluate subject mastery? Good question, and there is not a clear answer right now.

In the article "How trigger warnings could really work," Alyssa Rosenberg shared a portion of Angus Johnston's syllabus that he uses when teaching at City University of New York's Hostos Community College.

> "At times this semester we will be discussing historical events that may be disturbing, even traumatizing, to some students. If you are aware of particular course material that may be traumatizing to you, I'd be happy to discuss any concerns you may have with it before it comes up in class. Likewise, if you ever wish to discuss your personal reactions to such material with the class or with me afterwards, I welcome such discussion as an appropriate part of our coursework.
>
> If you ever feel the need to step outside during one of these discussions, either for a short time or for the rest of the class session, you may always do so without academic penalty. You will, however, be responsible for any material you miss. If you do leave the room for a significant time, please make arrangements to get notes from another student or see me individually to discuss the situation." (Rosenburg 2015)

Under this model, the student is still responsible for covering the subject matter, but not necessarily required to sit through disturbing videos or lectures. If it is possible to allow your students the flexibility to avoid certain lectures while still making them responsible for all material on tests or exams, you are likely in a good position to proceed.

However, if you encounter students who claim they cannot participate in any activity or subject matter because of triggers to the point where it might negatively impact their grade, you might need to find a way to work things out with the student. This could include helping the student unenroll from your class or assigning them alternative material that is at the same level of difficulty as the rest of the class work. The problem is that this violates the recommendations regarding consistency detailed earlier in this book.

The bottom line of this debate is to try to avoid connecting grades to areas that might come up with triggers as much as possible.

MISTAKE 90

Being too concerned about student evaluations when assigning grades to students...

I have heard more than one (non-tenured) professor complain about student evaluations. If your institution uses student evaluations to assess your performance, understand that you might not always like the overall result. However, you do not need to spend too much time worrying about them.

You need to allow your students the proper amount of privacy and data security when you have evaluations completed. Do not put any pressure on students regarding the outcomes of the surveys. While you want your scores to equal a high average, the actual numbers will not tell you as much as you might like about your students' experience. Instead, when you receive the surveys back from the school, go through the comments and see if there is any valuable feedback you can incorporate into your plans for the future.

Another important thing to review is what your students' were anticipating in regards to their grades. While you might not be able to pair up all the reviews to your individual students, you can measure the total of anticipated A's, Bs, Cs, etc... to the actual outcome. If they match up, at the very least your students have been able to accurately anticipate how they are doing in your course and will not be surprised when grades come out. On the other hand, if your students are anticipating grades that are very different from the ones they have received, you might have not done a very good job at communicating with your students in regards to their progress. This might be something to address in your future courses.

MISTAKE 91

Giving yourself too much work to grade...

Students often do not realize that when you assign work, they are not the only ones who have to spend time doing it. While providing your students with a ton of opportunity to learn is great, it is not the best if you can't keep up.

Never assign more than you can handle — if you do, you will not only be committing a disservice to yourself, but to your students as well. If you cannot handle the load, consider cutting back on how many classes you teach.

CHAPTER 13
Managing Distractions

Many things can prove distracting for students of any age, so much so that you might often wonder if your whole class is suffering from ADHD. If you thought all you would have to do is instruct students in your subject area – then someone lied to you. You will have the privilege of wearing almost as many hats as a parent.

You will, at times, have to deal with personality conflicts among your students. You should be watchful and prevent bullying and support students who are friendless. Finally, you will need to prevent anything in your classroom from becoming a popularity contest. This is quite a lot of social maneuvering for a teacher to pull off while trying to communicate the day's lesson. But if you do not fulfill these duties, then some students will get left behind academically.

You are probably thinking, *"I did not become a teacher to be a social director or a matchmaker or any other such nonsense."* Of course, you are correct in this regard, but if you are unwilling to dedicate some of your time to monitoring how your students relate to one another, you might not be able to maintain the order and structure your students need to thrive. Bullying, horsing around, and other petty relationship problems do not remain in the hall or common areas when students walk through your door; they impact your classroom as well. Be alert.

In addition to distractions that can occur from how students relate to one another, you may have to deal with distractions that come from high-tech devices such as phones, tablets, and game systems. If you are a recent graduate from college, then you will likely come from a world where you carry a smart phone and/or tablet with you at all times. You probably used it during your college classes and thought nothing of it – perhaps you even had a cell phone in your backpack in high school. Students having high- tech devices might not even faze you like it does others. But I can assure you, if your school has a policy regarding these devices, you should enforce it strictly. If you do not, then you should make a classroom policy for yourself and not waver from it.

Your classroom is not a place for smart phones or tablets. If your students have and carry these devices, you should ensure they keep them secured and put away, and that they are not brought out during class. Below are stories, advice and recommendations regarding dealing with distractions in the classroom.

High-Tech Distractions

As much as student interaction can cause distractions from the learning process, electronic items can cause the same problem. The most common sources of these distractions will likely be phones, tablets, and music devices. You might want to develop a strict classroom policy and communicate it to all students, and be prepared to back it up. Technology is wonderful and can, at times, greatly aid the learning experience. In fact, you can use high-tech devices to engage your students, but this practice should be in your control and under your supervision. Anything that falls outside of those parameters is more likely to cause problems than advance the learning process.

MISTAKE 92

Not having a policy about cell phones...

My personal opinion regarding phones and high-tech devices is that students do not need to bring them to class. However, personal electronic devices are necessary for many college students. Just because it is highly likely that all of your students own these devices, it does not mean that you should not require they are kept put away or on silent.

Your school might have a firm policy regarding high-tech devices. If that is the case, just enforce the school's rules. If you are allowed some leniency in this area, you will need to decide how much responsibility you are willing to shoulder in your classroom if you permit such devices.

There are a few things I believe you should consider if you decide to allow phones and high-tech devices in your classroom. First is the cost of such items if they are lost or damaged. You might consider this solely the responsibility of the student, however, maintaining an effective learning environment may require more attention than some can dedicate.

Another thing to consider is how secure your students' possessions are in your classroom. If your students sit and remain at assigned desks during your entire class, there might be no threat of theft. However, if your lesson requires students to keep their belongings away from their person, their possessions might become less secure.

Finally, you should consider what the benefit of having the device is versus the potential negative that could come from having it in your classroom. If the cost outweighs the benefit, adopt a policy accordingly. If you feel the benefit is worth a little bit of risk, adopt a policy that accounts for and seeks to minimize risk as much as possible and proceed from that point.

MISTAKE 93
Not having a policy about tablets/laptops…

So, do you allow your students to take notes on laptops or tablets, or do you require all electronic devices to be put away during your class? This is definitely not something you should be indecisive about. Make a policy, outline it in your syllabus, and stick to it for the entire semester.

If you are thinking of banning such devices in your class, you have hard research to back you up. Research has indicated that students learn better by taking hand-written notes rather than typing notes on a laptop (Hembrooke 2003). You would also not be alone. In a New Yorker article in 2014, Dan Rockmore, a Dartmouth professor, shared his long-standing ban on laptops and the more surprising idea that his colleagues in the computer programming department were echoing his sentiments (Rockmore 2014). The general consensus he shared was that students engage better, experience less distractions, and ultimately learn more when they are "unplugged" in the classroom. This is a compelling argument for banning electronic devices in your classroom.

Arguments against banning them seem to amount to "Let the students mess up and figure out what is best all by themselves." Or "policing the ban is too difficult." Perhaps that would be the case in a large lecture hall, but generally speaking, students are conditioned to follow rules. If you want to allow laptops or tablets in your classroom, feel free to do so. But do not permit them only because you think these students are incapable of putting them away.

While this is a minor consideration, please consider that depending on the setup of your classroom – and the availability of Wi-Fi – a student with a laptop or tablet might not just be distracting themselves from your lecture, but also students next to them. In the worst case scenario, a student sitting next to another could catch a glimpse of something offensive – like porn or a vulgar photo – and you have another can of worms to deal with.

Just remember that if it is reasonable to have students turn their phones on silent and refrain from texting, emailing, or taking calls during your class as basic etiquette, then it is just as reasonable to extend the same prohibition to other electronic devices. Whatever your policy is, be sure to define it on the syllabus and communicate it completely to your students.

MISTAKE 94

Not knowing exactly what to do in case of a fire, bomb threats, etc...

In the case of an emergency, you might be as freaked out as your students, but your class will likely look to you for instruction. Familiarize yourself with all of your school's standard operating procedures when it comes to emergency situations, know where your students should go, and be prepared to communicate instructions to your class if the need arises.

CHAPTER 14
Overcoming Outside Challenges to Learning

While it would be nice if every classroom was an island so outside influences did not distract from your teaching or students' learning, it's not reality. Some outside influences are internal to the student (such as learning disabilities), while others are external factors (such as a sick sibling or parents divorcing).

It is not your job to solve all of your students' problems. No matter how much you might want to, you probably will not be able to be their hero if things are going poorly at home. However, you can recognize if these outside influences are affecting a student's work and try to help them overcome whatever issues or challenges they are facing.

MISTAKE 95
Not tailoring work for a student with a physical or learning disability...

Should a student be diagnosed with a learning disability, tailoring their work to accommodate these concerns is vital to your success as a teacher and theirs as a student. Once you have been made aware that a student has a learning disability – whether at the beginning of the school year or later – you need to make any necessary changes that such a disability requires.

For example, you might have to administer some tests verbally instead of in written format for certain students. How much you need to adjust to accommodate a student's needs is different in each circumstance, but there is no question that you will need a plan.

In addition to students with learning disabilities, you might also have a co-ed with a physical disability of some type. For much of my life, I went to school with a girl who was deaf. While we were not always assigned to the same teachers, we did share many classes over the years. I watched her closest friends help her out even when teachers failed to communicate properly with her. She always comes to mind when I think about how a student with a physical disability has limitations that both the student and the teacher should work to overcome.

Schools have significantly more resources for students with physical handicaps than they did when I was young, but that does not mean you are off the hook for having a student with a disability in your classroom. It is important that you learn how to work with them to help them achieve their full academic potential.

In order to determine the best course of action for the student, you might need to consult with the student, other teachers, and school resources such as counselors. Follow the advice of your colleagues, and make sure you follow any laws or regulations that might be applicable in these instances.

MISTAKE 96

Permitting sexual harassment...

Considering you will be teaching a room full of adults, your classroom may not be free of loaded comments or advances. While it is not your place to prevent students from engaging sexually with one another, it is your duty to ensure your classroom is free of sexual harassment from both genders.

Neither your female or male students should be made to feel as if they are receiving unwanted sexual attention while in class. You need to be mindful of how students interact and respond to one another. If a man or woman seems like they are uncomfortable with how another student is talking to or flirting with them, you might need to separate those students.

Reminding students that they need to focus and be productive in class is important; however, you need to ensure that their learning environment is conducive for them to do so. Make sure your students know that you expect them to respect one another and that you will not tolerate harassing behaviors or displays of affection, whether they are wanted or not.

MISTAKE 97

Flirting with students...

Many people in their 20s have what I would call a flirtatious personality. As a teacher, you need to be mindful of the signals you could be sending to students with your smile, laugh, or even touch. You want to be sure you are not implying a level of intimacy that does not exist or a desire for a relationship that could get you arrested, fired, or both.

MISTAKE 98
Not dealing with a constantly sick student...

It happens to the best of us, and the worst part of being sick is when it does not go away. You may come across a student who has to miss huge portions of class due to a prolonged sickness.

If your student comes down with something like mono, or if they get into a bad accident and are subject to a prolonged hospital stay, it can be difficult to handle the situation in the classroom.

If you let the student miss a huge chunk of class time, you are disrespecting your other students who have made a point to show up for class. However, it can be difficult when you take into account that your student is physically and socially unable to make it.

In these cases, it is important to have an in-depth discussion with your sick student. Ask if they are able to continue on with the semester — it may be in their best interest to drop the class and focus on becoming well. If they insist on staying enrolled, you must set a limit. In general, missing more than 20% of the semester is where you have to draw the line. If they insist on staying in the class after that point, you need to refer them to the dean of students to further address the issue.

MISTAKE 99

Acting like sports do not affect your classroom...

If you are teaching at a major university, there is a good chance at least one collegiate sport (basketball, football, etc...) will be highly celebrated on campus. You can bitterly lament that athletics are so important at an institution of higher learning, or you can recognize that most alumni donations come in because of loyalty to school sports teams.

Alumni donations might be used to purchase computer equipment, upgrade libraries, or fund research. Therefore, the sports that you may find so unimportant might have a positive impact on your job. Ergo, accept the sports as part of your school's culture and work around them. Do not schedule tests on game days and do not be surprised if attendance takes a hit right before an important away game. You do not have to bend over backwards to accommodate sporting events, but working around them when you can will save you some headaches.

PART
THREE

RELATIONSHIPS

You might be wondering why a book about teaching mistakes would dedicate a large section of its pages to relationships. After all, why do relationships matter in an educational setting?

Simply put, how well you relate to your students and colleagues is just as important to your career as developing your students' knowledge and skills is. Even as you treat your students in an egalitarian manner, you will still form unique relationships with each one. One student might take away from your class a love for the subject matter while another may just remember your class as one they barely survived. The different details your students remember you for will be as varied as the reasons you remember them.

In addition to your student relationships, you need to be mindful of your relations with your colleagues and administration. Not only can other professors help or guide you when handling a difficult situation, but they can also help you advance in your career. Ignoring these relationships could hurt you when hiring and retention decisions need to be made.

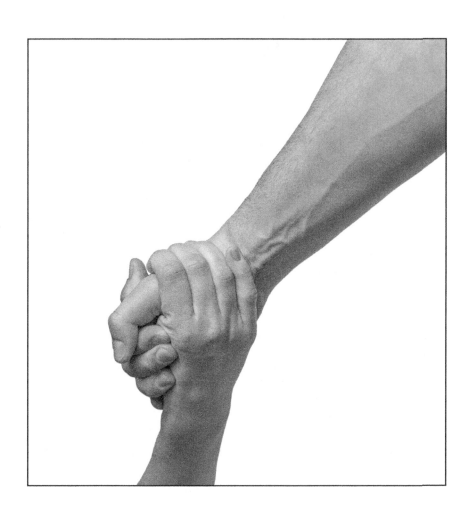

CHAPTER 15
Relating to Students who are Different from You

While they say that opposites attract when it comes to romantic interests, the truth is that in almost every aspect of your life you will find it easier to relate to those with whom you have shared interests or similarities. Shared history, fandoms, even something as small as being born on the same day or finding that you love the same movie can form the basis of a future friendship.

It is not surprising that you will find it easier to relate to students with whom you share common ground. The students who are different than you are the ones you may find the most difficult to manage, and not because they are poorly behaved or not teachable, but simply because you have more of a gap to bridge. This chapter is dedicated to helping you identify areas where you might need to work a little harder to ensure you are properly reaching your students.

MISTAKE 100

Continuing the Extrovert vs. Introvert war...

According to Jill D. Burruss and Lisa Kaenzig's article "Introversion: The Often Forgotten Factor Impacting the Gifted," most teachers report being extroverts. This is not very surprising since the school experience is designed to favor extroverts. From an introvert's perspective, the day is full of large classes and little to no opportunities to be alone and decompress. If a student carefully schedules their time, they can give themselves breaks, but they might not always be able to do so.

Try to remember that an introverted student is not just "shy" and in need of being "drawn out of their shell." On the contrary, they just need to be approached differently than extroverts. If it appears as if some students are uncomfortable in small groups, allow two-person teams to form. As long as an introverted student contributes to group work, do not discount their grade if they let another student do presentations. And try to remember to use methods that introverts respond to; some suggestions include independent study, small group instruction, collaborative learning activities, tiered instruction, role-playing, journaling, quiet time, and book clubs (Burruss 1999).

MISTAKE 101

Not understanding or respecting different religions...

In all likelihood, many of your students may identify as some form of Christian, though even on the smallest campus you will meet students from a variety of faiths and belief systems: Jewish, Muslim, Buddhist, Hindu, atheist or otherwise. Therefore, when you discuss holidays such as Christmas or Easter, try to remember other holidays that occur during the same time of year and try to be accommodating to students of other religions.

Should you have a student who is an atheist, he or she might prefer you refrain from any religious conversations or activities. If you need to discuss holidays or religion as part of your subject matter, try to do so in a neutral manner and present the material from as many perspectives as you can. This should protect you from perceived favoritism.

Finally, if you identify that one or more members of your class are from a minority religion, be sure to understand their traditions and accommodate student absence for their holy days (which may differ from traditional school breaks). While all of this might seem like a pain to you, being respectful of varying traditions in a multicultural society will benefit both you and your class.

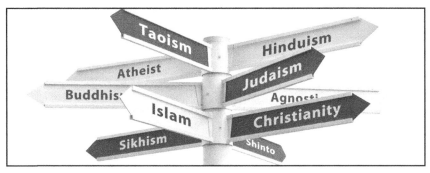

MISTAKE 102

Trying to impose your political beliefs on your students...

Political scientists looking to predict election outcomes have polled elementary-aged children on who they would elect president and found the correlation to actual results uncanny. The Scholastics News election poll has correctly called 15 of the past 17 presidential elections (Scholastic News Editors, 1996.). The simple conclusion is that children accurately reflect the political opinions of their parents, including thoughts about hot-button issues such as abortion, gay marriage, support for war, and immigration.

Even though you are teaching adults, these students probably carry political opinions they learned from their parents and might not yet be prepared to question or defend those positions. However, it is incredibly likely some students will be able to hold discussions on these topics. Should a student say something you strongly disagree with, I recommend not stating your personal opinion in the classroom, but instead play devil's advocate. If the students in your classroom express varying or opposing opinions, you can open the classroom up to discussion of the subject, but be sure to encourage polite debate, not flat out arguing. Be sure to never tell your class who you think is right or wrong.

The one exception to this rule is that you should correct opinions that carry a hint of racism or prejudice in order to make sure all of your students feel comfortable in your classroom. It is sometimes obvious when a student is a part of a minority group, however, it's important to not compartmentalize these students. You should remind your class that it is important to respect other people's religious beliefs, political affiliations, or culture. This could cause some conflict, but you need to stand firm and explain to them that you have students in your classroom from different cultures, and it is very important that you create a learning atmosphere free of bullying. Even if they do not like your stance, they will likely support it.

MISTAKE 103
Letting stereotypes show up in your classroom...

No matter what your life experiences have been, you need to make sure you and your students leave stereotypes at the classroom door. Even if the stereotype seems positive – like all Asians are good at math and science – it has no place in your classroom. You are there to teach students of all demographics and you need to create an atmosphere where each student can learn without the distraction of prejudice or bigotry.

If you approach teaching or allow your students to approach learning from a point of preconceived notions not based on performance, you will limit your students from the start. If you find yourself thinking a student will be good or bad at something based on nothing else but their gender or ethnicity, dismiss that notion completely and discover if the student is talented in that area or not.

MISTAKE 104
Treating men and women differently...

At the time this book was written, NFL athletes were making headlines for domestic abuse. It was an incredibly embarrassing time for the NFL as they worked out exactly how they should deal with the issue, and what punishment, if any, they were responsible for giving their players. One of the most common responses to the discussion about domestic violence is that a man never has a right to hit a woman, regardless of the situation.

Translate this idea to college students and you get the message that there is one standard for women and another for men. If you allow this mentality to seep into your classroom, you will encourage a dichotomy that does not facilitate a positive learning atmosphere and could lead to you getting a discrimination charge filed against you.

It is as simple as that. No matter what your personal opinion on this matter is, legally, you are required to create a classroom atmosphere where the genders are considered equal. Since that is your responsibility, I suggest that you dispose of ideas that say one gender can do this while the other cannot.

The more ways you can communicate equality between the genders, the less likely it will be that your students will come to think of an area of learning to be strictly for men or women. This will ultimately allow your students the best possible learning environment, and it should be your goal for every class you teach.

MISTAKE 105

Not protecting homosexual students...

College might be the first time that some students feel free to explore sexual urges they have felt all their lives. This means that gay students will transition past the point where they think of themselves as being "different" and start exploring their attraction to the same sex. Of course, recognizing an attraction is a long way away from living – and dating – as openly gay. However, some students may be at this point already.

Depending on the societal make up of the area in which you live, your experience with gay students could range from having an active LGBT+ organization on campus to an atmosphere that makes being open about one's sexuality seem impossible. No matter what your personal opinion is in regards to homosexuality or same-sex relationships, for legal reasons you need to take measures to protect all of your students.

Furthermore, in today's society, a student can be bullied by being called gay even if they have no such leanings. Make sure that you recognize when a student is being harassed and help them seek action if they need to. As society endeavors to create a gender-neutral world, or at least a world in which our differences do not exclude us from opportunity, you should try to make sure that students are not being made fun of because of antiquated ideas. By not allowing your students to perpetrate foolish ideas of what it means to be a man or a woman or attach negative feelings to the idea of being gay, you will do a lot to protect your students and your career.

MISTAKE 106

Allowing students to make fun of particular accents or cultures...

Some people will poke fun at anything they perceive as different, and unfortunately some adults never outgrow this mentality. A student who has a heavy accent or dresses differently because of their family's culture could be subject to ridicule or scorn. You should do what you can to put a halt to that type of behavior in your classroom and teach respect to all of your students.

MISTAKE 107

Assuming a student needs extra help if he or she is from another country or culture...

A good friend of mine, Sigmarie Soto, is from Puerto Rico, but grew up in the states. She explains that wrong assumptions hindered her academic advancement early on. "In first grade, I was assigned to a bilingual class because of, what I suppose, was an overflow of students. Although I am a native Spanish speaker, I learned to speak and read English at home with my mother. Because the students in this class were still learning how to read in English, I was going at a slower pace. For example, when the teacher would put us into a reading circle a few times a week, the allotted time would be over before I even got a chance to read."

If a lack of opportunity to participate was the only thing that came of this situation, it would not be so bad. But Sigmarie goes on to explain, "Close to the end of one of the semesters, my mother received a letter saying that I would fail first grade and that more specifically, I was failing reading.

My mother checked on this because I read in English at home all of the time and after talking to the principal and teacher, they had a third party come in and test me and a couple of other students separately. I ended up with above-average results on the test, but this could have been avoided if the teacher would have assessed the need and reading level of each student at the beginning of the year instead of making assumptions."

There are many lessons to be learned from Sigmarie's story, but I think the most vital point is that even if you hear a student speaking fluent Spanish (or some other language) outside your classroom, do not assume they are not fully bilingual and capable of excelling in English.

MISTAKE 108
Not using different teaching methods…

If you learn the best through lecture, that does not mean that your students do, too. If you graduated with a teaching degree, you are already well-versed in the area of teaching methods. However, for the sake of being thorough, it is important to have this in the forefront of your brain.

If you are in a rut of doing slideshows, switch it up and do a classroom discussion. Always integrate different multimedia methods, and keep up on the latest research in teaching techniques. Your students will thank you for ditching the monotone, boring standard and taking a leap of faith into the unknown.

It is worthwhile to ask your students how they respond to different teaching methods — ask them if they like lectures, slideshows, videos, discussions, writing time, etc. Also, keep in mind that every set of students is different.

Do not assume that you fall semester students will respond to your methods of teaching the same way that your spring semester students did.

Times change as well — the students of today have shorter attention spans than students of 50 years ago (thanks to technology). If something is not working, do not be afraid to change it up.

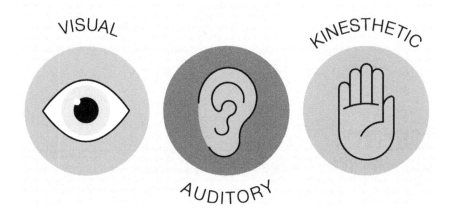

CHAPTER 16
Teaching Family

If you find yourself teaching in the town you grew up in, which is quite common, the chances that you will teach a family member at some point are high. The family member could be as close as your own child, niece or nephew, or more distant like your cousin's children. When this occurs, your first instinct should be to ask the school to reassign the student. If that cannot be accommodated, you should take precautions not to be perceived as unfair or biased.

MISTAKE 109
Not making administration aware of the relationship...

Of course, the first mistake you can make is not making administration aware of the relationship between you and the student. Even if classes are full, if staff is made aware of the problem, they can attempt to correct it. If no different accommodations can be made, at least your superiors and others are aware.

MISTAKE 110

Letting a relative call you by a name the other students cannot use...

If you do end up having to teach a family member, let them know that while they might call you "Aunt Trish" at home, in the classroom they need to address you as "Mrs. Robinson." You are not doing this as an attempt to hide your relationship with the relative from your other students, but just trying to leave the impression that all students in your classroom are on even ground.

MISTAKE 111

Working too hard not to show favoritism...

While you need to make every effort not to show favoritism to a family member, do not go too far in the other direction and become unnecessarily harsh toward him or her. Parents who coach their own children tend to vacillate back and forth between wanting to make their kid the star and being harder on their child compared to anyone else on the team. Your goal is to treat your family member the same as your other students, not better or worse.

CHAPTER 17
Relating to Other Teachers or Campus Staff

One of the most valuable assets available to a new teacher is other more experienced teachers. Chances are, no matter what shocking or challenging situation arises during your first year of teaching, one of your colleagues has experienced the same issue and will have some advice to help you handle it. Therefore, it stands to reason that forming and maintaining good relations with your fellow professors is an important part of your professional development. This chapter will offer guidance on mistakes to avoid in your efforts to create solid working relationships at your school.

MISTAKE 112
Not asking for guidance if you need it...

If you are reading this book, then you are clearly interested in avoiding mistakes. Your first year of teaching – well, any year of teaching, really – can be full of challenges and at times overwhelming. Many first-year teachers get burnt out and are just plain exhausted long before they get to summer vacation. If you get tired or frustrated, your students will suffer.

Do not be afraid to ask for advice and use it (and sick days; you get to use those too when you need them).

One of the biggest mistakes inexperienced teachers and professionals alike make is wanting to cover up their inexperience so much that they do not ask for help from their colleagues or supervisors. Your coworkers and supervisors can help you and in many cases, they have quick, easy advice to give you that can make your life easier. Ask questions, seek guidance, and leverage your associates' ideas so you can be better at what you do.

MISTAKE 113
Getting involved in campus politics...

Schools have their own versions of office politics and getting involved in them can prove detrimental to any teacher, but especially so to the new guys on the block. Just as your students might have squabbles, grudges, and backstabbing, your coworkers probably do too. The best action you can do is to steer clear and stay quiet.

If there are instances where you have a vote in a matter, listen carefully to what others have to say about the individuals up for a position and participate in the election, but do so without drawing attention to yourself.

MISTAKE 114
Not valuing department staff and technical resources...

The department secretaries can be very useful resources to you. Some of them have worked at the college or university for many years and can help you with scheduling issues, unpredictable student needs, and other problems that will arise in your first few years of teaching.

Technical resources on campus will support you in everything from grading to email communications to recording your final grades. You should know what help is available to you and who you can contact at any given point in time (many colleges have technical support personnel that provide 24/7 on-call support).

They can also advise you on teaching ideas that are not practical. For example, systems administrator David Allan West at the University of Florida pointed out issues pertaining to printing and large classes with 30 or so students. He suggested that instead of each student attempting to print a copy of their paper before they leave class, email their assignments to the professor instead. This will help the professor avoid technical issues such as printer jams, paper/toner/ink running out and delays in classroom turnover.

If you plan to use networks or systems in your teaching, be sure to review their capabilities with the technical support team assigned to your building. They can be invaluable to ensuring your class plans run smoothly.

MISTAKE 115
Getting caught up in gossip...

Like any work environment, gossip will circulate at school. People will discuss each other's personal lives, professional behavior, and at times cross lines that should not be crossed. While technically talking about anyone behind his or her back can constitute gossip, there is definitely positive and negative talk. Discussing how you love someone's idea for a fundraiser is vastly different than speculating why someone's husband never comes to school events.

While it might seem like listening to campus gossip is an easy way to start to fit in and bond with your coworkers, it could prove detrimental to your working relationships or even your career. Even if gossip seems harmless, it can lead to you getting caught up in the campus politics mentioned in the previous entry and make you someone that another teacher now has a grudge against.

As you will recognize with your own students, your reputation will be shaped by the company you keep – so just listening to someone else gossip can hurt you. Find a way to politely excuse yourself from conversations when this sort of activity comes up. Do not be concerned about what people will say behind your back when you leave the room. Just conduct yourself as you should, and soon you will earn the respect of your colleagues.

As an addendum to this mistake, do not gossip with other teachers about students or parents. OK, yes, students talk about you and parents probably do as well. And yes, by the time I graduated high school, I realized that teachers talk about students and parents, too. It takes place in just about every teaching lounge across the country. However, it is still best to avoid it because of the problems it can cause. And if you are new, it is far more likely to hurt your career than help it.

MISTAKE 116

Passing along a false allegation...

One of the worst side effects that can come from gossiping is passing along a false allegation, whether the allegation comes from a student, parent, or another teacher. If it is something that should be brought to a principal or supervisor, do it and then wait and see what happens.

Reputations can be damaged in an instant and take an eternity to repair. Even being vindicated from a false allegation cannot always repair a damaged reputation. While there are some things that cannot be ignored, it is best that you do not help convict someone of something before all the facts are known. If a teacher is accused of misconduct, abuse, sexual harassment, and other inappropriate behavior, your best course of action is to make the necessary report and let management take action. Just understand that accusations are not always true and spreading gossip will not benefit you if turns out to be a false report.

If, after watching management's course of action, you decide the situation was handled badly, you might need to make some decisions about going over your supervisor's head or going to the school board. But that is a worst-case scenario that you will hopefully never face, especially not in your first year of teaching. Even in that case, gossip will not help you. You might need to seek advice, but do so one- on-one with someone you respect and trust.

CHAPTER 18
Connecting with Students

Connecting with students can be really difficult. Not only are you in different places in your lives, but there is also a teacher/student dynamic. Being accessible to your students while still maintaining a respectful demeanor can be a challenge.

One of the most rewarding things you can do as a professor is to form a relationship with your students. Not only will you undoubtedly learn something valuable from them, but you will also gain knowledge about another life. Depending on what your specialty is, this information can be extremely useful for you.

This can also make teaching a pleasure — relationships are, after all, the zest of life. Without further ado, let's take a look at some mistakes teachers make when it comes to connecting with students.

MISTAKE 117
Not getting to know your students...

It is not always necessary to get to know your students, but it can make the teaching and learning processes a lot simpler and easier. Invite your students to come into your office to introduce themselves.

Often times, students do not realize how many other students you are teaching — let them know that it can be very valuable for them to visit you and offer up an introduction. Once you can attach a face to a name, you will find that your feedback and emails to your students can be much more personable.

If you develop a relationship with a student (we are obviously talking about a professional relationship here), you can also have the pleasure of seeing how your influence has formed them. Nothing is more rewarding than receiving an email from a past student letting you know how much of an impact you had on their success.

You may also find that students are more likely to interact with you. Students may come across an interesting article and send it your way, they may stop to chat in the hallway, or they may even stop by your office with cookies.

It does not matter what you are trying to get out of the situation — the simple fact is that developing a professional and respectful relationship with your students will enhance both of your life experiences.

MISTAKE 118
Letting your religion get in the way...

Many of us are not people of the same faith. Even among those who practice the same faith, there are variations of denominations. While I understand that some religions teach their practitioners to live their life as a witness, evangelizing in the classroom is a mistake — it can get in the way of being able to connect with your students. It is possible that it could get you fired, as well.

If you lecture on religion, be sure to use facts, not opinion. It is always best for you to present history in terms of facts and let your students draw their own conclusions. Otherwise, you build a wall of resentment and hate between yourself and your students.

There is no way you will be able to connect with your students on a professional level if they are blinded by your personal beliefs.

MISTAKE 119
Not allowing for casual conversation...

You may be skeptical of this one, but keep in mind that many students are going through things that you are not aware of. If you jump right into a lecture and never allow time for some casual conversation, you are not allowing yourself to connect with your students.

Beyond simply creating a relationship, this also forms a welcoming environment — a place where your students feel safe and included. This goes back to not knowing what they are going through — it can be an amazing thing to know that your classroom is a safe haven for an abused or harassed student. Even a student that feels lonely can benefit from a classroom that allows for casual conversation. If someone asks you how your day was, and no one has asked you that for a long time, it can have a profound effect on your overall well-being.

Also, getting your students talking with casual conversation can help them feel more comfortable when it comes to classroom participation. If they know their other classmates and are used to speaking up, they may be more likely to raise their hand and answer that challenging question.

A good way to include casual conversation in the classroom is to allocate a specific time for it. Perhaps this is the first five minutes of class; you might ask your students in general if they did anything fun over the weekend, you might talk about the latest in film or television show, you might talk about that newest scandal in the news... as long as you engage your students in some kind of casual conversation, you are going to help develop all of those positive outcomes.

MISTAKE 120
Not attending extra-curricular activities...

While you will not have time to be a part of everything, it can be a huge help to go to an outside event or two during the semester. Always know your limits, and never attend an event if it is going to cause you unneeded stress.

However, if you can manage it, doing so can be a huge help when it comes to connecting with your students. If you expect your students to appreciate what you love, it is important to reciprocate that feeling by appreciating what they love.

Students are happy to see teachers at outside events, whether it be a football game, a musical, a poetry reading, a presentation, or a seminar. You will most likely be greeted with smiles and waves from your students. Being actively involved with the events of your institution should never backfire on you as long as you keep up with your job requirements. It will also provide fodder for casual conversation in the classroom — "Who else went to the football game on Saturday night?"

Not only does this benefit your connection with your students, but your coworkers and authorities will be pleased, too. Nothing impresses your boss more than going above and beyond by being actively involved. Make a point to block off your calendar at least once during the semester.

MISTAKE 121

Not telling personal stories...

Let your students get to know you. They are more likely to open up to you if you open up first. This is the easiest, most natural way to make a genuine connection with your students.

It does not have to be a particularly noteworthy story — just let your students in to your life every once in a while. Tell a story about your pet, your parents, or your significant other. Inject some humor into your usual routine.

MISTAKE 122
Not including classroom discussion...

In other areas of the book, we briefly cover the importance of hearing different voices speak in the classroom. However, this is another great way to connect with your students.

When you allow students to speak up through a classroom discussion, you not only help them to form and project their own opinions and ideas, but you get to know them a little better. The learning environment that a classroom discussion provides can be priceless in many ways — your students are working on defending their positions, building their own authority, and in some cases, just learning to speak in a public setting.

If you dedicate some class time to open discussion, you can prompt your students to choose the topic, as well. This gives you additional insight into who they are, and it can help you connect with your student's interests.

MISTAKE 123
Not helping students from poorer backgrounds keep up with the class...

Be mindful of differing financial backgrounds before you send home assignments that require even small purchases. If a student tells you that he or she could not complete an assignment because they did not have the supplies, be sympathetic and provide them with an alternate opportunity.

Students will come to resent you if you assume that they have extra money to spend. You will not always be able to supply your class on your budget, but be aware that your students (and especially their parents) have budgets, too, and some of them are incredibly tight.

Always be aware of possible financial issues, and work with your students by offering to lend a copy that you own or supplying them with rental or library information. Money seems to get in the way of everything, but do not let it get in the way of connecting with your students.

CHAPTER 19
Serving as a Reference

One of the earliest challenges you might face in your teaching career that you may not anticipate is having a student ask you for a letter of recommendation. The most common letters of recommendation you will be asked to write are for entry-level corporate positions, internships, or graduate schools. No matter how much effort you take to get to know your students, writing a letter of recommendation will likely require reaching beyond your knowledge of the student and drawing connections between what you have seen in your classroom with what a hiring manager or admissions board wants to see.

You can draw these connections from the person's academic work, community service, academic/school achievements, or work study/part-time employment. In each case, the key is to make sure you know enough about the student to provide them a solid letter of recommendation. But before you agree to serve as a reference, read the following recommendations and decide if you should proceed or decline.

MISTAKE 124

Not knowing the difference between the professional letter of recommendation and the academic letter of recommendation...

The professional letter of recommendation is defined as a letter written for someone looking to be hired at a new company or promoted internally into a new position. You might be asked to write this type of letter of recommendation for a student who is getting ready to graduate and is looking for their first job or for a student applying to an internship.

The first thing to understand about writing a professional letter of recommendation is that you are, generally speaking, addressing the person's ability to do a job and/or perform in a work setting. You should not speak to areas of the person's abilities that you are unfamiliar with. Instead, highlight the professional skills you have seen the person demonstrate strongly.

Remember, you are probably not the only person the candidate is asking for a letter of recommendation. When each letter states the candidate's strengths from each person's point-of-view, a strong picture is painted for the reader. There is no need to oversell the person, just promote the aspects you are familiar with.

Conversely, the academic letter of recommendation might be written for a student's initial acceptance into an institute of higher education or be used for someone seeking an advanced degree. In your role, it is likely you will only be writing letters for students who are seeking admission into graduate school, law school, or medical school. You could also be asked to write a recommendation for someone pursuing a scholarship or other funding to continue their education.

These letters can profoundly impact someone's academic career, their professional future, as well as their ability to pay for their education. Thus, these letters are important and a little more varied. Rather than just speaking about the person's ability to do a job, you need to address their ability to take on a challenge and succeed.

Each person who writes a letter of recommendation used for academic purposes might not be familiar with the student's grades or academic qualifications. That is OK, because that is not all an admissions board is considering. They also want to know if the person possesses leadership qualities, if they are well-rounded, and if they will contribute something to the student body other than just tuition dollars. This is particularly true of advanced degrees. While you have an idea how the student performed in your class, try to touch on any observations you have made about these other qualities as well.

Let me reiterate again how a mediocre letter of recommendation can hurt a person's candidacy for a job or academic program. If you do not write the letter of recommendation from the right point-of-view, you could hurt the person's candidacy more than help them.

MISTAKE 125

Writing a letter of recommendation when you cannot positively endorse the candidate...

There are several things you should consider when you decide whether or not to agree to write a letter of recommendation. There are several reasons why you might just need to say no. The absolute most important reason you should decline serving as a reference is if you cannot say great things about the candidate with a clear conscience.

There is a chance that the main reason the student asked for the letter of recommendation is that you seem nice and they did not think you would turn them down or say anything damaging about them. Another reason they might have asked you is because you have some connection to the job or internship and they want to leverage your relationship to boost their chances of getting hired or selected.

These are valid reasons to ask someone for a letter of recommendation, but do not feel like you have to agree. In fact, do not agree if you do not feel comfortable saying something positive about the student. Since the standard for listing someone as a reference is to ask them first, hopefully no one gives out your contact information without checking with you. If you do get blind-sided by a call, be kind and honest and let the person know later that you do not want that to happen again.

Since you will mostly be requested for letters and you cannot be caught by surprise in writing a letter, do not waste your energy writing a bad one. In fact, do not even write a mediocre letter of recommendation. Readers will be expecting very positive endorsements and a lackluster one is as bad as a negative letter. Understand that by failing to write a good, strong letter of recommendation, you could subject yourself to potential legal ramifications if you sabotage someone's job or academic pursuits.

While it can be difficult to bring a defamation case to trial and win, you probably do not want to subject yourself to one. If the subject of your letter learns that if not for your statements, they would have been hired or accepted, they might have a case for damages. Yes, they would have to prove that you knowingly wrote a bad letter, but why take the risk? If you cannot say something positive about a person, just politely decline to write the letter.

MISTAKE 126

Writing a letter of recommendation if you do not know enough about the person to endorse them properly....

Sometimes people, students in particular, are not really sure who to ask for a letter of recommendation. They might ask a college professor who seems nice, but can barely remember them. Therefore, one reason you might want to decline serving as a reference is if you cannot remember the student from Adam. If you can recall nothing about this student, do not try to make it up. If you can do no better than writing a vague letter for a person, explain to them why you are not the best person to endorse them and perhaps help them think of someone better suited for the task.

Remember that some of the things you will need to cover in a letter of recommendation include an evaluation of a person's work ethic, his or her ability to meet deadlines, perform under pressure, how well he or she works with others, and what type of culture the person excels in. It is not a good idea to put anything in a letter that you cannot back up during a phone call. Therefore, again, if you need to decline because you do not know the candidate well enough, do so. It would be better for them to seek a different reference than for you to write an incomplete one.

Finally, note that some professors like to tell students to write the letters themselves so they can just sign off on them. Do not do this. When you endorse someone through a letter of recommendation, you are putting your professional judgment up for consideration. You do not want to earn yourself a reputation as someone whose endorsement means nothing, or as someone who will sign off on whatever a student gives them.

MISTAKE 127

Agreeing to write a letter of recommendation if you do not have time....

Many academic institutions have deadlines for submissions and require letters of recommendations to be mailed directly from the writer. In instances like this, a person cannot ask for a letter from you that they can use on more than one occasion. Even employers might make this same kind of request. If you do not have the time to write a powerful letter in the timeframe a person needs the task completed, do not add this to your never-ending to-do list. Just tell the person you do not have the time right now, and encourage them to come to you next time with more time before the deadline.

The academic letter of recommendation is a diverse category that spans from undergraduate college admissions to law school and medical school. The complexity of evaluations and hurdles students must overcome vary in difficulty as well. In a highly competitive market for admissions into top schools, and even seemingly less competitive schools, letters of recommendation can make a strong impact on acceptance or rejection.

MISTAKE 128

Not knowing what rules or guidelines the letters of recommendation need to meet....

Letters of recommendations may or may not be requested of an applicant. Often, they are just something the person thinks will serve them well in professional pursuits or something the person needs to assemble for school applications.

However, there are times when the letters of recommendation need to follow very specific guidelines for content, deadlines, and methods of submission. If the letter needs to be mailed in a sealed envelope by July 1st to be considered, you need to make note of those requirements and adhere to them if you agree to write the letter.

MISTAKE 129

Not knowing who you are addressing the letter of recommendation to or the purpose of the letter...

While some job candidates and school applicants will ask for letters they can use for multiple applications, others will need them addressed to specific hiring managers or committee members. In these instances, you will want to address your letter to an individual, not a generic recipient (i.e. Dear Sarah Marshall or Dear Hiring Manager).

Even when you do not have a specific person to address, you can still customize your letter to companies or schools if you know the focus of the individual's job or academic pursuits. This is important because you might mention certain achievements above others if you know what the reader will find the most interesting or valid.

MISTAKE 130

Not including information that specifically speaks to the job or program the student is applying to...

In continuation of the concept above, if the subject of the letter can provide you an actual job description or details about the university or program they want to attend, you can write a more targeted letter. In these instances, you can select key words from the job description or program website to plug into your letter. These descriptions can also give you guidance in what achievements or qualifications you can note about the subject of the letter.

After you have acquired this information, you can begin drafting the letter and planning what you are going to say about the recipient. If you determine through this information gathering process that you will be unable to meet a deadline or some other rule for submission, inform the person immediately so they can ask someone else to write the letter.

MISTAKE 131

Not knowing what needs to go into a letter of recommendation...

One of the first things you will want to do in a letter of recommendation is explain your qualifications and why the reader should place significance on your endorsement. In the process of introducing yourself and explaining your relationship with the subject of the letter, you will need to qualify yourself to the reader. In other words, convince them that they are interested in what you have to say.

As Steve Elcan, a regional sales director for Oracle, explained to me, "The most important thing to me is who the letter of recommendation is from. I want to know that the person writing me has some firm ground to recommend this person for the position I am interviewing them for. I care more about what the CEO of an IT company has to say than the CEO of a bakery."

While I have explained that anyone can write a letter of recommendation, as Steve points out, the reader will want to know why what you have to say matters. So while this letter is not for promoting yourself, highlighting your qualifications can help enhance your endorsement of the subject of the letter.

Since your relationship with the subject of the letter is mainly academic, you can speak about coursework and mastery of subject matter, but you can also go into how the person performed on academic projects or in classroom activities such as speeches or small group discussions.

Example:

> *"William was an excellent student and always delivered his work on time and to the highest quality standards. He did more than just master the course material; he was a constant leader in group discussions and helped fellow classmates understand concepts they missed during lectures. A couple of weeks into the semester, he took the initiative to organize student-led study sessions that greatly benefited those who participated.*
>
> *My opinion of William is that he is more than just an excellent student, he is also a natural organizer and team leader. This is backed up by his position as captain of a student intramural basketball league and membership chair of his fraternity. As he progresses in his job*

duties, I have no doubt that he will find opportunities to help his team members improve in their performance while delivering at peak levels himself."

Or:

"Ashley is a naturally gifted speaker and she always appeared at ease when addressing her classmates for presentations. She would communicate the facts of her presentations with in-depth knowledge and answer questions from her classmates with confidence. When called upon to participate in classroom discussions, she provided interesting insight to the material and could draw upon her knowledge of news and current events to deepen the discussions.

Ashley did well in my class, but I saw much more in her than a mastery of my subject material. She demonstrated a passion for the subject area, and I have been informed by her other professor that she brought the same energy to his classrooms as well. I believe she will continue to pursue education and training in this area and should prove valuable to you as she progresses in expertise and ability."

In addition to promoting a student's academic work, you can also talk about school achievements. Even if the student had to make you aware of these things himself or herself, it is reasonable that you can cover those accomplishments in your letter.

Be it winning a scholarship or earning a starting spot of the school's basketball team, a school achievement can convey several skills that hiring managers want to see in their candidates. You can talk about a person's school achievements and tie it into their academic work if you are a professor, resident director, or organization sponsor. This should allow you to give a more complete assessment of the candidate beyond your direct involvement with the subject of your letter while still staying within the body of experience the reader will expect you to cover.

Example:

> *"As Matthew's speech and English literature instructor, I had the privilege of witnessing his commitment to coursework firsthand. He was an inquisitive learner who frequently went above and beyond in his assignments. His speech work was particularly exceptional as he presented information effectively and powerfully.*
>
> *However, the thing that impressed me the most was how Matthew did so well in my courses while maintaining his basketball scholarship. The demands for his time between his courses and athletics left little time for socializing I am sure, but he continued to excel at both. I believe this demonstrates a talent for time and resource management that will prove valuable in his professional pursuits."*

Or:

> *"My experience with John was as the College of Journalism's faculty director for student government. John served as the secretary and later president of the organization. During his tenure, he effectively represented the school to the larger university governing body while shaping policies that positively impacted the school.*
>
> *During this time, I know John maintained a grade level that qualified him to graduate with honors. I have spoken to several of my colleagues in the College of Journalism and they all speak highly of his dedication in the classroom and work product."*

MISTAKE 132

Not properly tailoring the letter for graduate programs...

A graduate school candidate might be looking for admissions immediately after completing their four-year degree or they could be a professional looking to expand their knowledge and capabilities. Therefore, they might request a letter of recommendation of academics or professionals. It is key that the person who writes this letter has direct knowledge of the work and the character of this applicant.

You do not need to attempt to write a letter for someone who you knew several years ago and your familiarity with their work has significantly decreased. Just because someone is applying to a school program does not mean they need letters of recommendations from academics. It is important that you do not commit to writing a letter if you don't have a number of positive things to say about the applicant.

One of the most important things to remember about grad schools is that they are not just looking for students who will do well in the classroom. They are often looking for people who can work as teaching and research assistants, and bring recognition to their program with their future achievements. They might also be looking for individuals who have new research ideas and show promise for being published. With that said, it is important to promote what the individual can offer the program and their fellow students as well as what they can do academically and professionally.

MISTAKE 133

Not providing the right information for a student applying to internships...

Some might consider an internship an entry-level position because they are compensated with course credit instead of payment, which is why I decided to include it in the academic portion of this book. Letters of recommendation for internships can be completed by both professors and current or former part-time employers, but they need to speak to both academic and professional traits.

Internships are very important because they help new graduates present professional qualifications when they enter the job market at large. A letter of recommendation for an internship will help hiring managers choose from dozens or maybe hundreds of applicants. While you will want to talk about their academic success, I recommend you focus on other highlights in order to distinguish them from their competition. Consider:

- The candidate's future work goals

- The candidate's passion for the subject of the internship

- The candidate's achievements outside of academia (work or community service)

- The candidate's organizational skills, ability to deliver on a deadline, etc...

- The candidate's ability to do the internship (link what you know about the candidate to what you know the internship will require)

MISTAKE 134
Not providing a means for follow-up...

One final note regarding the content strategy: It is important to make sure the reader knows they can contact you if they have any additional questions about the candidate. Whether or not they call you is not the important thing; it is vital that you communicate that you are more than happy to talk about the candidate further. The fact that you are willing to speak about the subject of the letter in greater detail tells the reader you are fully committed to endorsing that person. Be sure to include a valid phone number and email address in the header of the letter, closing paragraph, or both.

NOTE TO READERS: On the following pages, I have provided a few samples of letters of recommendation you can use as models for endorsing your students.

Academic Letter of Recommendation from a
Teacher/Professor (Graduate Program, Political Science)

DR. STEVEN MONROE

555-555-5555 | Street Address, City, State, Zip | smonroe@university.com

(Date)

Mr. (Ms.) _____
Title
(Company)
(Address 1)
(Address 2)

Dear Mr. (Ms.) _____

It is my pleasure to write to you on behalf of Melody Burger, recommending her for your graduate program in Political Science. My first impression of Melody came as a stand-out student in a large lecture for American Federal Government. I had the opportunity to get to know her better in my Presidential Politics course her junior year.

Even though Melody was majoring in journalism, she excelled in her political analysis, research, and studies. She made thoughtful and insightful contributions to class discussion, indicating that she did more than just the required reading for the course. Additionally, I found her paper submissions to be comprehensive and high quality, particularly her submission on the relationships between the media and presidents' press secretaries.

Since Melody expressed an interest in political campaigning, I recommended her for an internship with a local candidate. His feedback on her work ethic and contributions was excellent and he served as a source for her honor thesis on impartial media coverage of politicians and parties.

I highly endorse Melody for your graduate program and believe she will prove an asset to your university. If I can provide you with any additional information or be of any further assistance in your consideration of Melody's candidacy, please feel free to contact me at the phone or e-mail listed above. Thank you for your time and consideration.

Sincerely,
Dr. Steve Monroe

Academic Letter of Recommendation from a Teacher/Professor (MBA Program)

SUSAN MICHELLE ROBERTS

555-555-5555 | Street Address, City, State, Zip | susanmichaelroberts@university.com

(Date)

Mr. (Ms.) _____
Title
(Company)
(Address 1)
(Address 2)

Dear Mr. (Ms.) _____

Benjamin Taylor has asked me to recommend him for your school's MBA program and I am glad to do so. For three years, I had the privilege of sponsoring State University's Business School Student Counsel where Benjamin served as Treasurer and Vice President. Additionally, I instructed him in Macroeconomics and Statistics.

Benjamin excelled in my courses and in his upper class academic pursuits, maintaining a GPA that qualified him to graduate with honors. However, I had the chance to get to know Benjamin better outside of the classroom due to my work with the student counsel. In addition to working on student policies, the counsel has led several job fairs and new student orientations. Benjamin proved himself to be an excellent project planner and event leader.

Four years ago, Benjamin was hired by a large consulting firm and my connections at the company tell me he has excelled in his efforts there. Having gained a great deal of hands-on experience, Benjamin now wants to complete his MBA and begin a transition into management. I believe he is a natural leader and will excel in these pursuits.

As such, I strongly endorse Benjamin for admission into your MBA program and will gladly provide additional information about his qualifications and achievements if needed. I appreciate the time you have spent reading this letter. If I can be of any additional assistance, I can be reached at 555-555-5555 or at susanmichaelroberts@university.com.

Sincerely,
Susan Michelle Roberts

Academic Letter of Recommendation from a Current or Former Teacher (Internship)

DR. SAMANTHA JONES

555-555-5555 | Street Address, City, State, Zip | jones_samantha@emailaddress.com

(Date)

Mr. (Ms.) _____
Title
(Company)
(Address 1)
(Address 2)

Dear Mr. (Ms.) _____

I am writing to you on behalf of Bill Smith to recommend him for your summer internship research program. For the last two semesters, Bill has worked as my teaching assistant for Intro to Biology and Human Anatomy 101 at State University. From what I have observed of him as my assistant and what I know of his academic and professional work, I can fully endorse his application to your program.

I first met Bill when he was a student in my entry-level courses and I advised him in selecting his academic path during his sophomore year. As a TA, he is organized, helpful to the students, and capable of adjusting to challenges that present themselves throughout the semester. I can entrust Bill to proctor exams and lead effective review sessions with dozens of students. He will make an effective instructor himself someday, but his real passion is in research.

In addition to his assistance in the classroom, Bill has also been helpful with lab work and analysis that I and some colleagues are conducting on platelet rich plasma (PRP) therapy for wound care. Bill is quick to take on extra work on this project and has contributed to some of our findings. Prior to assuming the position of my TA, Bill volunteered at the local hospital to familiarize himself with the daily happenings of a hospital environment.

For all of these reasons, I believe Bill will excel as a researcher and your internship program should provide ample proving grounds for his skill sets. Additionally, I believe you will benefit from his work product. If you need any additional information regarding Bill, please feel free to contact me at the phone number or email listed above.

Sincerely,
Dr. Samantha Jones

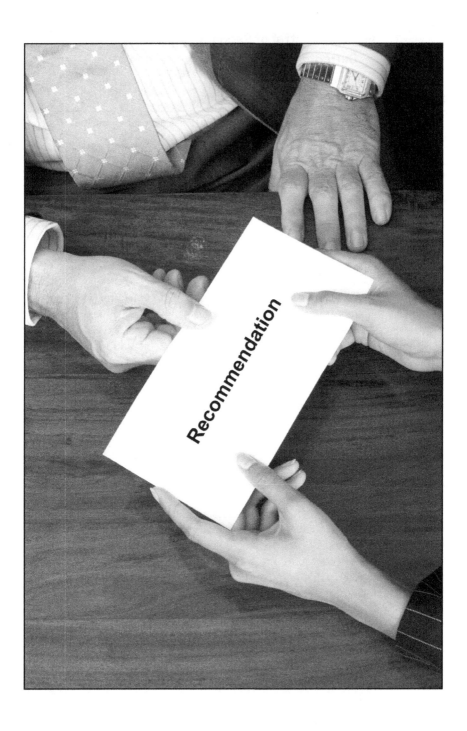

PART
FOUR

CHOOSING YOUR
SCHOOL ENVIRONMENT

If you are reading this book while still conducting your job search, part of your consideration should be to factor in the type of teaching environment you want to work in. If you have already accepted a position, you should be continuously aware of the fact that different teaching setups face different challenges. This section is dedicated to issues you might face in specific academic environments.

CHAPTER 20
Challenges Adjunct Professors Face

Making a living as an adjunct professor can be challenging. In most instances, you will be paid a certain amount of money per class at two intervals throughout the semester. I have read reports or articles written by adjunct professors who taught multiple courses at different colleges in order to make enough money to support his or her family.

This could mean a great deal of community, several sets of superiors to answer to, and very tight schedules to adhere to. As states face budget limitations and schools experience hiring freezes, relying on adjunct professors is a good way for universities to ensure they can offer classes. However, these arrangements are not necessarily permanent and ultimately lead to the instructor feeling overworked and underpaid.

If on the other hand, you are a full-time professional who happens to add to their income by teaching one or two courses as an adjunct professor, you face a different set of challenges. The first and more difficult challenge is giving your students the attention they need while managing your normal work commitments. Read on to identify mistakes to avoid in this work setting:

MISTAKE 135

Not communicating well with students even though you are not on campus much...

While you might not be sure when you want to see students or even when you can see them, you need to have open lines of communications with your students even if you cannot have definite office hours. Communicating with your students via email, through a school website, or even through a social media platform such as Twitter might be even more essential to your success than to professors employed by one university.

It is very important that your students feel like they have access to you outside of the classroom. And it is important for you to be able to address individual student concerns outside of your classroom so that your lecture does not get derailed too frequently. Though it might be difficult, if you can arrive at your class a little early or stay a little after to address student questions and concerns, that will ease the burden of not being able to host office hours. However, you might face scheduling conflicts with the space that is available and have to encourage students to contact you via email or by phone.

Even if you cannot schedule open office hours, try to be available to meet with your students by appointment. You also need to provide your students with contact information that includes your cell phone if you are not frequently available for communications in any other manner. I remember frequently having professors' cell phone numbers, but typically the only time I needed one was when dealing with adjunct professors. When I worked as one myself, I provided students with my cell phone number (but not my house phone).

You need to maintain a certain amount of privacy in regards to your students while providing them with solid lines of communications. For example, if you are a big user of social media, you might want to consider leveraging Twitter to provide your students with updates regarding your class or curriculum. However, I would advise against connecting with your students on Facebook as that might be too close to fraternizing. However, there are some cases where Facebook can be a valuable tool, such as having a class group page.

MISTAKE 136
Taking on too many classes...

If you are making your living solely through teaching, you might be tempted to take on as many classes as you can. But try to recognize that if you do this, you are creating a heavy burden for yourself not just in teaching, but also when it comes time for testing and final exams.

If you are teaching several courses at different institutions, be sure to carefully schedule test dates, papers, and projects so that you can provide them all with sufficient time in terms of grading and meeting with students. You will need to chart this out at the beginning of the semester, but careful planning will prevent you from over-tasking yourself during peak testing periods.

MISTAKE 137

Making grading too hard on yourself...

The last thing you want to do is put yourself in a situation where you have hundreds of essays to grade from hundreds of students spread across multiple colleges. To make things easier on yourself, schedule your due dates in a staggered manner. That way you can dedicate one week to grading papers from one class at one institution and another week to grading assignments from a different class at another school.

MISTAKE 138

Acting as if one class is more important than another...

While you certainly do not want to be the last priority of any of your students, it is true that for some, you might be less important to them than other courses. However, as a professor, you should never let any of your classes or students feel this sentiment coming from you.

If you find yourself thinking that one class you are teaching is easier than another, you could find yourself putting less effort into teaching it. Just because the subject matter seems easier to you, that does not mean your students will not find it challenging. If you are taking on many courses as an adjunct professor, make sure you give each class your full focus and attention.

MISTAKE 139

Not giving your courses as much attention as your "day job"...

If you are working as an adjunct professor, but working another job as the main source of your income, you need to be sure that you are giving your students the same effort a full-time professor would give them.

Students can gain a lot of understanding from instructors with real world experience, but not if you treat your class like it is your last priority. I have had many professors who were tasked to teach us specifically because of their day jobs. The benefit from their experience and list of contacts was essential to many students in our department who were trying to find their first job. Obviously, none of these professors treated us as if we were not a top priority for them.

CHAPTER 21
Challenges New Professors Face at Major Universities

The challenges a new professor will face at a major university can be much more significant than if they decided to work at a smaller school. Making tenure is far more difficult, and publishing is expected rather than desired. The pressure to perform at a major university is much higher, but you might find there are many more opportunities to gain recognition in your field. Whether or not you are comfortable in this environment might depend on how much you enjoy publishing or competitive settings compared to how much time you want to spend with family, or if you prefer working in a less-stressful work environment. Hopefully, you will have a chance to decide ahead of time which atmosphere you would prefer. If not, be sure to review this chapter for mistakes to avoid at a major university:

MISTAKE 140

Neglecting your students so that you can do research...

Being a faculty member at a large institution means that you are expected to constantly be immersed in your craft. From publishing requirements to tenure, you are expected to be up-to-date with the latest research.

The whole concept of tenure is that you will be rewarded based on works you have published, which effectively rewards the time you spend researching over the time you spend actually teaching your students.

While it is very important that you do research and work toward being published (see the next mistake), remember that your job is to teach. Do not neglect your student's education so that you can get ahead with research. Instead, find a balance between teaching and researching. Integrate your research into the classroom and discuss your latest findings with your students.

Whatever you decide to do, remember what your main objective is — to teach students and to do it to the best of your ability.

MISTAKE 141

Not publishing...

Of course you know the adage of "publish or perish." Therefore, you know the importance of doing research, fostering ideas, and putting forth new topics for publication within your field. As I have already mentioned, it can be beneficial to team up with already established professors and leverage their connections to advance your own work. You can also build on the success you had in publishing your thesis or dissertation. The important thing is to continue with your publication efforts without putting them on the back burner while you focus on your class instruction. Try to find the balance between these two efforts as they are both vital to your career and advancement.

MISTAKE 142

Not partnering with colleagues on papers or presentations...

Teaming up with a colleague comes with the downside of having to share credit for your work, but it comes with many upsides. The benefits range from making publishing an easier feat as previously mentioned to helping you balance your course load with the need to keep your name appearing in academic and industry journals.

By teaming up on papers and presentations, you might be able to advance higher quality work rather than pushing sub- par submissions to journals just to try to keep up with the expectation of your institution. Since you are early in your career, you might believe that quantity matters more than quality, but focusing on producing good work that is well-received will benefit your career more in the long run. If you need to team up to achieve this, the benefits far outweigh the downside of having to share credit on your work. This also demonstrates that you are capable of successful collaboration.

CHAPTER 22
Challenges New Professors Face at Community Colleges

At a community college, you might not be required to publish as much as you would at a major university. In fact, your focus will likely be consumed with teaching multiple, diverse courses. The challenges you face have likely been detailed throughout this book already, but I want to draw your attention again to some mistakes you can make in a smaller school environment.

MISTAKE 143
Being inaccessible...

Community college students often need more access than traditional four-year students. They may benefit from email updates and reminders, a time for questions during class, or an overall more accessible demeanor. Keep in mind that your students may need some prodding as well.

Invitations to attend office hours and encouragement to make an appointment when there is difficulty learning might be what some of the students need in order to get their questions answered. You may find that students shy away from seeking additional help, so it is in everyone's best interest to constantly remind them that you are accessible

During class, always ask if anyone has questions. At the end of class, remind your students of your office hours. In personalized emails, let any struggling students know that you are available for appointments, and if need be, ask a student to meet with you.

Keep in mind that if you come across as severe or intimidating, your students will feel that you are inaccessible, and they will not seek the help they desperately need.

MISTAKE 144

Becoming more lenient...

While many students excel while in community college, it is still true that the admissions process is far simpler. This means that you will most likely be teaching students who are not as college-ready as you may be expecting.

Professor David Sack, professor at Lincoln Land Community College in Springfield, Illinois, said, "There's a huge pressure to lower standards, but there's also pressure from administration to pass more students, because they get money from the state for students completing their degrees. I try to give the same level of difficulty year after year."

MISTAKE 145

Promising a positive outcome to students...

Working for a community college can be very different from working for a big university — especially considering the overall environment. Typically, community colleges reflect a more personable environment. There is a higher emphasis on catering to the individual, and more precautions are taken to ensure that each student is being served according to his or her needs. Because of this environment, it can be tempting to promise a positive outcome to students.

Many teachers feel the need to reflect the personable and caring environment that a community college evokes by saying something like, "I promise that with hard work and dedication, you will make it through this semester just fine."

This kind of sentiment effectively promises a passing grade to every student, regardless of whether or not they have the necessary skills and abilities to earn it. It is important that you not let the community college environment affect the standards you have for your students. Never promise a passing grade to anyone, especially at the beginning of the semester.

MISTAKE 146

Becoming overly frustrated with a student's lack of basic reading, writing, and mathematical skills...

Some students who attend community college cannot properly write complete sentences or understand how to follow basic instructions.

Professor Sack elaborates, "I have had some of the smartest students you'll ever meet, but I have also had students who can't write a simple sentence."

Since many community colleges have open admission, students that lack basic reading and writing skills are not turned away. It is acceptable for a professor to show disappointment, but if a student or group of students feels attacked by a professor's frustration, they probably will withdraw and disengage from the instructor, creating a bigger problem.

These students might also opt to talk with the dean of students — whether you are in the right or wrong, the dean of students might choose to side with the students, putting you in an awkward position as a new teacher.

Do your best to work with your students, and if the problem is severe, suggest tutoring or ask them to seek additional help and guidance. You also must be open to helping students during your office hours. Suggest that they set up a time to meet you to go over a particularly difficult section or topic.

CHAPTER 23
Teaching Graduate Students

There have been a few times in this book when I have made notes on the difference between teaching undergraduate students versus graduate-level masters and doctoral candidates. In almost all cases, there will be differences in how you work with and interact with graduate-level students. After all, they may eventually become your colleagues and some of them might even start developing and leading their own courses while they finish their dissertations. As this transition is made, you will want to make changes in your relationships, but be mindful to do this only after it is clear you will not be teaching these students in the future. Read on for mistakes to avoid until that day comes:

MISTAKE 147
Relaxing boundaries with graduate students...

There will undoubtedly come a moment when you feel like telling older graduate students to call you by your first name, especially if you are close in age. While in the U.S., we are not as formal as other cultures in this regard, there is an unspoken rule that addressing someone by their first name denotes a level of familiarity that once achieved, is not easily reversed.

As I was completing my master's degree, I watched several PhD candidates struggle with how to refer to professors who they worked closely with on a daily basis. There are professors that to this day, I still remember as "Dr. So- and-So" rather than "Steve."

If you believe you have passed the point when you will be teaching an individual or if you believe your graduate students would benefit from a more relaxed learning environment, pay attention to how your colleagues are addressed by their students and try to imagine if your approach will earn you the respect of your colleagues. If the answer is no, adjust your strategy accordingly.

One strategy you can use to decide how to permit students to address you is to pay attention to how tenured professors refer to each other when talking to students. If they commonly call each other by their title and last name, they are probably reinforcing an idea of authority rather than familiarity in the department. If that is the case, you should follow their lead and adopt a more formal tone with your students. If your colleagues seem to operate in a more informal manner, you can follow suit, but do not feel like you have to. It still might be a good idea to not be too familiar with your students until you have earned a more solid space on campus.

Just remember that while you can always tell a student down the road to call you by your first name, it would be impossibly awkward to ask a student to switch to a more formal method of address once a casual relationship is established.

In the same regard, when you are associating, traveling to professional conferences, and participating in department activities with graduate-level students, the issue of fraternization can become blurry. As much as you deem necessary, you need to create and maintain strong boundaries for socialization with your students – even graduate students.

However, if you are part of the same social circles as some of your students or somehow see your students in some other social setting, there might come a time when you can develop a more familiar relationship. Just be mindful of when it is appropriate to make that transition.

MISTAKE 148
Not asking for feedback...

As a new teacher, it's important that you ask your students for feedback. In the case of graduate students, it is arguably even more important, because their education is at its peak. Not only are they paying more money for your time, but they are honing in on their specialty — it is extremely important that you get their education right.

Not to say that asking undergraduates for feedback isn't important, but in most cases, the actual teaching methods you use with graduate students will be different. The classes are often smaller, and you're on a more personal level with your students. If something you are doing in the classroom is not working for your students, they may not feel like it is appropriate to bring it up.

This is why it is really important that you start a dialogue about feedback — specifically ask your students what is and what is not working for them. Are your multimedia components helpful? Do they like the classroom discussions? Is the lecture time productive, too short, or too long?

It can be helpful to make the feedback inquiry anonymous by dedicating a short period of time at the end of class to allow your students to write down their thoughts. Have them turn those papers in to you at the end, perhaps in a jar, and make it known that they should not put their names on the papers. The best way to be a better teacher is to ask your graduate students for feedback. They have been in school for a while, and they have a general sense of what is expected of them. You are not likely to receive unwarranted comments about too much homework as you might with undergraduates.

MISTAKE 149

Asking graduate students to do things at the last minute...

If you need 100 copies of a test made and you have a teaching/graduate assistant whose job it is to do this for you, make sure you give them plenty of time to complete the work. By asking for things to be done at the last minute, you will annoy your support team and make them less likely to want to help you. Even if the graduate assistant has to do what you ask, they will probably start to share their negative opinion of you with other graduate students. This may eventually reflect poorly on you. It is best to be considerate of your graduates students' time.

MISTAKE 150
Overloading your teaching assistant...

"As the professor, you (or your grader/TA) has to fairly grade every assignment. If you give a large number of assignments, your TA may start just grading to get it over with and not hold a high standard. You need to make sure you are not overloading yourself or your TA," said Shannon Bow O'Brien.

If you assign too much work, your teaching assistant might end up being lazy in his or her grading, which will likely lead to grade inflation because the TA is unlikely to fail students just because he or she is tired of grading work. Rather than inflate grades needlessly and fail to measure if the students are mastering the subject matter, assign less work and make sure you or your TA has time to evaluate it carefully. This will help keep you, your TA, and your students from burning out.

PART
FIVE

PROFESSIONAL MISTAKES TO AVOID

As a new teacher, you probably have a one-year contract at most. No matter how secure a teacher's position with tenure may be, you could do your job perfectly and still not be renewed the following year. Follow the advice in this section to give yourself the best shot at a more permanent contract.

CHAPTER 24
Behavioral Mistakes

Throughout this book, we have covered several things you should not do. But this chapter is dedicated to compiling in one place several mistakes you could make in regards to how you behave on the job. If you can avoid these mistakes, you should be able to prevent any serious issues of discipline or reprimand.

MISTAKE 151
Using language not fit for the classroom...

I dedicated a section to how you should avoid cursing in front of your students, but you should probably avoid inappropriate language at work altogether. While I am sure many teachers will use more adult language in their break room, it is probably best that you try not to flip back and forth between knowing when you can and cannot say certain things.

Note that there are words that might not be considered "curse" words, but they should still be excluded from your vocabulary completely. From racial slurs to gender-specific insults, you probably already know the words and phrases you should avoid. Remember that just like there is appropriate attire for work and "going out" clothes you can wear with your friends, your language needs to follow the same rules. Just because you use a word with your friends and do not think anything of it, does not mean you can speak like that at work. When in doubt, err on the side of caution.

MISTAKE 152
Showing prejudice or bias...

Just like any professional environment, you have to comply with certain standards and expectations. One of the biggest ways you could get yourself in trouble is to demonstrate racism, sexism, or any other bias that could be perceived by your students or coworkers.

You should assume there is no safe prejudice you can demonstrate in the workplace. We live in a far more diverse world than before, and even the smallest towns may have students who observe unique religions, are from small, not well-known foreign countries, or have parents of the same gender. No matter what your opinion is on race, religion, gay marriage, or nationality, you should make it a point to not make disparaging remarks to your students or coworkers about any minority group.

Furthermore, in your efforts to minimize harassment in your classroom, it would be best for you to lead by example and not make jokes at anyone's expense. When a student sees you crack a joke at someone's expense, they may think it is safe for them to do so. Being careful in this regard will set the right tone for your classroom and protect you professionally.

MISTAKE 153

Cold-calling...

When you call on a student that isn't ready, not only are you setting up your students for failure, but you also cause them to fear the classroom, which is supposed to be a positive learning environment.

You want your students to feel like the classroom is a safe place — not only safe in terms of violence or harassment, but safe in the respect that they can voice their opinions and be themselves. When you demand that a student respond to you in an instant, you don't allow for time to collect his or her thoughts. Every person is different — just like not all people are leaders, not all people are able to think fast.

If you want to build a classroom environment that is welcoming, inspiring, and educational, it is important that you ditch the cold-calling and come to accept silence. While silence can be awkward at times, it can produce the most thought-provoking discussions, and at a far greater level than any cold-calling will.

MISTAKE 154

Over-preparing...

While being prepared for a lesson is really important, it is possible to be too prepared. Finding the balance is key.

If you come into the classroom with notes on every single point you want to discuss, you might end up boring your students. We all know that reading material from a piece of paper is never a good idea, but even structuring a lesson too tightly can be constrictive to your student's educations.

Allow room for development – let your students guide some of the discussions. Instead of structuring a lesson around a specific passage, consider doing a chapter instead. Instead of jotting down 15 specific conclusions to discuss, jot down 10 ideas. Then, let your students fill in the blanks.

If you come to class too prepared, your students will be bored by the monotony. You will come across as rigid and stuffy – not that you should particularly care what your students think of your personality – but the problem is that you are jeopardizing the education of your students.

If they would rather take a snooze than participate in your class, it is possible that you have over-prepared.

MISTAKE 155
Not watching yourself teach...

This can sound a little creepy, but stay with me. Everyone has quirks. It can be anything from the way you stand to a phrase you say over and over again. We rarely notice our quirks (sometimes we do), but the ones who are really noticing it are your students.

When you constantly say the word "so," your students get distracted. You should worry less about them making fun of you and more about them missing your main point because they keep waiting for you to say "so" again. The real troublemakers might even be sitting in the back counting how many times you say it.

Other teachers get less caught up with words and more caught up with body language. Perhaps they keep running their fingers through their hair, maybe they constantly scratch their nose, or maybe they clear their throat obnoxiously.

Whatever your quirk may be, there is a chance that it is affecting your student's ability to learn. While it may seem less important than, say, avoiding a lawsuit, it should be a top priority for you.

To figure out what your quirk is, you can do a variety of things. You can first ask people that are close to you. It may not be the best idea to ask your new colleagues, because you could be putting them in an awkward situation. They may know right away what your annoying tic is, but letting you know can make them feel uncomfortable. Try asking a significant other or a family member.

Secondly, you can ask your students. This has the potential to be awkward as well, but if you have a naturally laid back feel with your students, they may not feel uncomfortable about discussing the topic.

The most valuable thing you can do, though, is to record yourself teaching. This sounds less than fun (or maybe not), but teachers are not the only ones that do this. Most performers watch themselves perform to recognize any flaws in their performance. While you are not exactly Beyoncé getting ready to perform in front of millions, you are still performing.

You are a speaker, and with that responsibility comes recognizing your shortcomings. Make sure to record yourself teaching at least once. It can be a valuable tool for figuring out your quirks, and you can explain the importance of this to your students.

MISTAKE 156

Asking to meet outside of your classroom/office...

The way you act in the classroom is one thing, but if you purposefully create an opportunity to act differently outside of the classroom, you run into risky business. It does not matter what your intentions are – perhaps you ask a student to meet you for breakfast so that you can discuss their presentation – anything and everything can come back to bite you.

You may feel like you know your student well, but if you do not, they could use the outside meeting in a very damaging way against you. You could potentially lose your job, face disciplinary action, or even face a lawsuit for harassment or sexually related charges.

Beyond possible job loss or legal trouble is the fact that your request could be taken in the wrong way, not only by the student in question, but by other students, parents, and coworkers. This is particularly true if you ask a member of the opposite sex.

If you have a need to meet with a student outside of the regular classroom hours, do it in your office or in an appropriate place on campus. A good general rule of thumb is to imagine telling your mother what the plan is. How do the following scenarios sound? 1) I asked my student, Claire, to come in to my office to discuss her senior thesis. 2) I asked my student, Claire, to join me for dinner and wine to discuss her senior thesis.

Be conscious of how you act around your students, and to protect yourself, never meet outside of the classroom or your office.

MISTAKE 157
Getting political...

If you are a new hire during an election year, that is probably not the right time for you to be overly vocal about your political opinions or who you are supporting in local school board elections. I am not saying you need to bite your tongue forever when it comes to politics. However, I am suggesting that when you are new to a work environment, you have no way of knowing who is friends with whom. The last thing you want to do is express negative opinions of someone who wins an election to someone who knows that candidate.

When it comes to politics – local and national – my advice during your first year of teaching is to listen to the opinions of those around you without overtly stating your own. Particularly when it comes to school board or superintendent elections, take the time to get to know why your fellow teachers support one candidate over another. Listening to your colleagues may help you form or reform your own opinions while ensuring you do not leave a negative impression on those who know more about the school district and personnel than yourself.

MISTAKE 158
Dressing inappropriately...

Your school likely has a dress code for you to adhere to and there will be scheduled days for casual wear. However, you should likely do more than meet the dress code early in your career. Career coaches have loads of advice to share with candidates on how to dress for interviews. I have heard of people not getting a job simply because they did not meet a certain standard for interview attire.

It is almost disturbing to think that qualifications can be damned if a dress code is not properly met. However, in today's market where there are more qualified candidates than job slots, every bit of distinction can separate one person from another. During your first year, you are in many ways still a job candidate.

Therefore, it will probably serve you well to dress a little nicer than required throughout the school year. There will certainly be times when wearing a school T-shirt and jeans is more than appropriate, but otherwise, dress up rather than down.

MISTAKE 159

Dating someone on the staff...

Of all the places a single person can meet someone to date, work is the number one location for most. However, dating someone in the workplace is usually frowned upon, even in the corporate environment. At a school, you might have fewer opportunities, but it is an equally bad idea.

If you meet someone at the school, date, and eventually marry, everything could come up roses. However, if you end the relationship at some point, it could create a very awkward work environment for both of you. As a new teacher, you do not need to add stress to an already stressful job. It is for the best that you keep your work and personal life separate and date outside of the school.

MISTAKE 160

Refusing to change...

If a method you're using isn't working, the worst thing you can do is to try harder. Often times, new teachers will become discouraged when a particular teaching method or disciplinary method isn't working – instead of trying harder, opt to try something new. The chances of it working are much higher. .

MISTAKE 161

Accepting gifts from a student or their parents...

You might not think of a student bringing you flowers or handing you a bottle of wine at the end of the semester as a bribe, but you do not want to allow that to become a perception of those who observe this behavior.

If you see a student outside of the classroom – with or without their parents – do not allow them to buy you a drink or dinner or anything else that might imply you will need to view the student in a favorable light later.

Whether these gifts become known to other students, and the person who gave them to you appears to receive a benefit from them or you simply find yourself in an awkward situation where you have to give a poor grade to a student who has given you things, this practice can be bad for your career. In order to avoid having to explain something to your boss or face litigation, just decline any gift a student wants to give you.

MISTAKE 162

Not reporting illegal behavior...

As a teacher in any environment, you will likely witness a whole slew of bad behavior, ranging from bullying to drug deals. In the roughest of schools, problem individuals might exercise certain methods to intimidate not only students, but also teachers. However, you need to take the necessary steps to protect yourself legally. Therefore, if you witness illegal behavior, you need to report it. No matter what threats, bribes, or pleas come your way, it is ill-advised to turn a blind eye to behavior that should be brought to the attention of your superiors. Failing to do so could make you the subject of a lawsuit and/or get you fired.

MISTAKE 163

Drinking or smoking at school...

There will likely be a designated smoking area at your school for the teachers. In many states, it will be outside because of laws regarding smoking in work environments or public facilities. While it is permissible to go outside and smoke during your breaks, if you can avoid it you might want to consider doing so.

The recommendation not to drink at work should be a no-brainer. However, there was at least one teacher at my high school that was rumored to have a flask in her desk and her breath reportedly smelled of liquor throughout the day. Do not put yourself in that situation as it would undoubtedly cost you your job.

CHAPTER 25
Continuous Improvement

As a teacher, you are a life-long learner whether you like it or not. You will be called upon to complete several hours of professional development throughout your career and be expected to continuously work to improve your performance in the classroom. You might as well begin this process in your first year of teaching and perhaps impress your boss in the process.

MISTAKE 164
Not working on your classroom presentation skills...

Hopefully you are an eloquent speaker who does not get tongued-tied or find yourself at a loss for words. However, if you still need to improve your lecture or presentation skills, be sure to practice this as the year goes on. I am certain that you will be observed at times to evaluate your performance. When this happens, you want to make sure you are comfortable leading your classroom and are free of verbal pauses and lapses. Since practice makes perfect, work on this with friends, in front of the mirror, and perhaps even ask a mentor to observe your classroom before your evaluation to provide tips and recommendations.

MISTAKE 165

Not planning ahead...

In the first chapter, I reviewed how important it is to plan for the first day and week of school, but that is not where the advance planning ends. You will want to plan weeks in advance for delivering your curriculum and planning tests or special projects. You need to take a look at the school calendar and see how to fit your curriculum plan into the school schedule to make things easiest on the students. You do not have to have a plan so firm you never deviate from it – just make sure you are not making it up as you go along.

MISTAKE 166

Not adjusting your lesson plan if needed...

If something comes up that you failed to anticipate, make sure you are willing to alter your lesson plan to accommodate needed changes. Whether this is due to students needing more time on the material or an interesting learning opportunity arose that you want to take advantage of. While it is vital to plan ahead, it is also important to be flexible enough that you can always put educating your students first.

MISTAKE 167

Not adjusting teaching methods that appear ineffective...

Since you are new to teaching, it is reasonable that you will need to make changes to your teaching strategies throughout the year. There may be nothing wrong with your approach in theory, but it could just not work for you and your students. Whether this is a change in testing strategies or trying a new approach in how you communicate a lesson, be open to trying something new if it will help your students better master the material they need to learn.

MISTAKE 168

Not reviewing what types of questions your students are struggling with...

Every time you give a test, you have an opportunity to evaluate where your students are struggling at an individual level and also as a group. If you find that most of your students are having a hard time with a specific type of problem, you should spend extra time reviewing that material and practicing how to answer those questions. If all you do is grade the tests and give them back, you miss an opportunity to improve your teaching approach.

MISTAKE 169

Not reading the work of your colleagues or reading in general...

As busy as being a professor will keep you – whether you're grading papers or working on your own research – it is important to keep up with work your colleagues are completing as well as local and global events. Being in a workplace that focuses on academics and growing personal knowledge, it should be a given that you should make it a personal goal to learn as much as possible every day, as well as teach. This includes keeping up with not only school-relevant news but also other current events that may prove as important elements of discussion among your peers and students.

MISTAKE 170

Avoiding committees...

While it is not advisable for you to take on more than you can handle in your first year of teaching, if asked you should not avoid serving on some department committee. You might want to consider not serving on a graduate student's committee or a hiring/search committee until you have been teaching for a few years, but I doubt you will be asked. When the time comes for you to serve, agree to one committee at first to learn the function and add to your responsibilities over time. Avoiding them altogether will only make it look like you do not want to be part of the department and will do little to impress your supervisors.

MISTAKE 171
Avoiding department activities...

While you do want to avoid campus politics, that does not mean you want to avoid department activities altogether. You should willingly attend lectures, presentations, luncheons, and other events hosted by the department. This will allow you to get to know your colleagues and help you remain up-to-date on what others in your field are studying, researching, and publishing.

MISTAKE 172
Not having a short professional bio on your webpage...

Building and updating your biography is an important part of your career management. A biography can be written in first or third person and should cover some of your most recent work first. This can include the name of the university where you are employed, courses you are currently teaching, and research you are working on.

Additionally, you might want to include a summary of prior professional experience and educational highlights, including one or more of your degrees and institutions you graduated from. You should also include highlights of speaking engagements you have completed, recent or most prominent publications, and positions of leadership you have held in professional organizations.

Finally, you can include some personal notes regarding your spouse, family, personal interests, or hobbies. This part can be left off, but if included, it should be limited to just one or two lines.

Creating and keeping your bio up to date will allow you to submit it easily if a conference or publication wants it and allows your students to know a little about you prior to taking your class. While that might not seem vital to you, some students do enjoy knowing a little something about their professors background and credentials before they take a course from them.

MISTAKE 173
Not maintaining your CV or resume...

It is always important for you to update your resume or curriculum vitae whether you are on a job hunt or not. You may want to include it on a university or college web page or simply have it as a reference document when you are making a presentation at a conference.

However, it is a huge professional mistake not to simply have your career management documents up to date at all time. Whether you take advantage of an internal position or a job opening at another institution, trying to assemble a CV at the last minute can be daunting. If you are unsure what to include, focus on the following:

- Summary of your qualifications
- Your credentials and educational background
- Your employment history, including details regarding the courses you have developed and taught
- Committees you have served on, particularly ones you have led or chaired
- Languages and special skills
- Technical skills

- Professional associations and memberships
- Presentations you have made
- List of publications

An educational resume or CV does not need to follow some of the standard rules of resume writing, including limitations to two pages. Please see the following pages for some formats to use:

CV Sample

- First Name Last Name
- Phone
- Email
- Address – city, state, country

Title:

Three to four line summary detailing your area of expertise and course instruction experience.

Career Achievements:

*Include four or five bullets in this section that highlight your accomplishments.

These could include a summary of courses you have led, a listing of journals in which you have been published, or a list of committees you have served on/chaired.

Education:

*Include your degrees from Bachelor's to PhD along with titles of papers you have published. It is not necessary to include year of graduation, but you can unless your years of completion go back too far. You probably want to leave years off if it stretches back more than 20 years.

- Name of Institution
- Degree
- Title of Dissertation
- Name of Institution
- Degree
- Title of Thesis

*Additionally, you might want to include certifications in this section and change the header title to "Education and Credentials." If not, you can move this information to the second page of the resume with your specialized skills.

Professional Overview:

*In this section, you want to include roughly 10-15 years of experience.

- NAME OF EMPLOYEE
- **Title**
- Years of Employment
- Bullets summarizing your duties and responsibilities.
- Bullets describing special achievements.

- NAME OF EMPLOYER
- **Title**
- Years of Employment
- Bullets summarizing your duties and responsibilities.
- Bullets describing special achievements.

- NAME OF EMPLOYER
- **Title**
- Years of Employment
- Bullets summarizing your duties and responsibilities.
- Bullets describing special achievements.

*You can include a career note at the bottom of this section that summarizes earlier professional experience without years.

Specialized Skills:

*This section can include language proficiencies and technical skills.

*You can also include information in this section regarding special credentials and certifications if you leave them out of your education sections.

Awards & Distinctions:

*This section should include information about any awards you have received. If you have graduated recently, you can include fellowships and other financial awards for your studies.

Membership & Associations:

*This section should be a list of professional associations you have joined, any title you have held with those groups, and committees you have served on.

*If you have specific accomplishments you want to share while part of a professional association, you can include it here.

Publications & Presentations:

*This can be a partial or full list of presentations, posters, conference appearances, and publications that you have delivered over the course of your academic career. These should be listed in reverse chronological order starting with your most recent work first. As you advance in your career and your earliest work ages past 20 years, you should consider removing it.

*If your list is very long, you can concentrate on your most recent work, and also your most important accomplishments.

CHAPTER 26
Avoiding a Lawsuit

It is almost a shame that I have to include a chapter like this, but it is also easy to get sued in today's world (or at least threatened with it). In order to protect yourself against litigation and disciplinary measures by your administration, avoid the mistakes laid out in this chapter.

MISTAKE 174
Not knowing applicable laws for schools in your county and state...

Ignorance of the law is not a defense for breaking it. This common axiom is the reason why saying you did not see the speed limit will not save you from a ticket. Breaking the law at your school as a first-year teacher will undoubtedly make it difficult for you to advance your career. Make sure you know the laws and regulations that apply to your school and make every effort to comply with them.

MISTAKE 175

Not making students aware of risks, even ones you think they should know...

As foolish as it may sound, if you fail to make students aware of potential danger and they get hurt, you could be considered liable. Therefore, put some thought and consideration into what dangers your students may face in your room and what safety rules you need to brief your students on. This is especially prevalent if you are working in a lab setting.

MISTAKE 176

Not monitoring your students' safety while they are in your care...

If you are in the science field, you need to make sure all of your students are exercising proper safety procedures. If your students get hurt while failing to comply with safety or good laboratory protocols under your supervision, you could be held accountable. Be careful about allowing yourself to be distracted for an extended period of time, or focusing so intently on an activity that you lose track of what is going on in your classroom.

MISTAKE 177

Purposely embarrassing a student...

I have detailed how being snide, sarcastic, or rude to a student is unprofessional and unlikely to achieve your purpose. However, you should be aware that embarrassing or harassing anyone on purpose is also a good way to get yourself reprimanded or named in a lawsuit. If you are ever tempted to speak harshly to a student (no matter how justified it may seem), be cautious, bite your tongue, and keep silent.

MISTAKE 178

Not removing or reporting a student who proves dangerous to another student...

You know that you need to maintain a safe, bully-free classroom. If you feel that a student is starting to pose a danger to another child, do not ignore your gut feeling. Ask the student to leave your classroom if necessary. Hopefully, your superior can take the needed steps to get the aggressor in line so that there are no instances of violence. While some old-fashioned parents might not blink an eye at a couple of boys getting into a tussle, many parents today would be very upset if their child was hurt at school. Do not let any such incident happen on your watch.

MISTAKE 179

Not protecting a student's privacy...

In an earlier chapter, I advised against engaging in gossip in regards to department staff, coworkers, or fellow professors. When it comes to your students, you should always aim to protect their identities as this is likely school policy and/or law in your state. If you want to seek the advice of a mentor and explain the problem you are facing with a student, do so without naming names. In the instances where it is necessary to discuss the student by name, be sure that you are doing so for the good of the student.

When it comes to protecting student privacy, you must protect everything from their grades to their private data. You need to be careful not to reveal social security numbers or school identification numbers to anyone else. Failing to do so could subject you to a lawsuit or complaint.

MISTAKE 180

Not complying with laws regarding suspicious behavior you must report...

There are instances where you learn, or think you have learned, information that you are required to report to the appropriate authorities. If you think you are obligated to report something, but are unsure how to do it or who to contact, consult someone at the school who is qualified to advise you – a school psychologist, a mentor teacher, or your superior.

MISTAKE 181

Not knowing your students' medical needs...

Hopefully your students do not have overly complicated medical needs, but if they are facing severe allergies or other potential health risks, you need to be aware of them and know what to do in the case of an emergency. This is especially true if you are going on a field trip with your class. Do not take it for granted that all of your students are healthy as a horse – make sure you review their files for any information you need to remember throughout the school year.

MISTAKE 182

Using a student's image without their permission...

This is pretty simple and straightforward – do not use images of your students without permission. Do not post their images in your newsletters or on a social media page. Do not use their image in any way without first getting signed permission.

MISTAKE 183

Being negligent...

If you see something happen to a student, you are required to help or report it. For example, if a student gets injured – say they trip on campus – you are required to help them or alert medical services.

The past few years have produced some pretty horrible court cases that could have been avoided if the teachers had not been negligent. In January of 2012 in Illinois, a young student slipped on a mound of snow, hit his head, and broke his leg. The school staff allegedly told him to crawl back to the building because they couldn't carry him and did not have a wheelchair. They did not call any medical services. The boy's parents filed a lawsuit asking for $200,000 in compensation for the cost to treat his injuries, missed time at school, and pain and suffering.

When you're officially a new teacher, it is of the utmost importance that you are vigilant and take charge of situation such as this – if you are seen as negligent, you could be facing a judge.

MISTAKE 184
Making assumptions about students...

The larger the school you are teaching at is, it is obvious the students you encounter will be that much more diverse. I have covered a variety of mistakes when dealing with diversity so far; however, it is important to reiterate that student appearance may have nothing to do with their performance or even true personality.

For example, there are a lot of assumptions about students in Greek life or other organizations on campus, and it may be hard to avoid adopting these assumptions. If a student sports letters or represents a group that may have certain connotations, it is important to evaluate him or her individually. Some Greek chapters are perceived to have members that party too much, participate in illicit activities, or are just all-around questionable individuals. It is important to ignore these stigmas.

In many ways, college is an incredibly free environment with much fewer rules than many students are used to. Even if a student has a lazy-looking wardrobe, they still may be among the brightest in the room.

MISTAKE 185
Showing physical displays of affection with students or a teacher...

No matter what age of student you are teaching, physical displays of affection or comfort need to be done cautiously and sparingly. The same rule applies to your teachers and coworkers. I do not want to believe we live in an age where you cannot hug a student or coworker who tells you that there has been a death in their family or some other upsetting news. But you do need to be cautious of the risk of being accused of sexual harassment. What seems innocent to you could be perceived as unwelcome physical contact to someone else. The best policy is probably a complete hands-off approach; otherwise, my best advice is to proceed with caution.

MISTAKE 186

Failing to accommodate the accommodating...

It is often that students may have jam-packed schedules spread across large campuses. This might make it impossible for certain students to get to your class on time, or remain in class for the entire block. Even though having someone enter or exit in the middle of your lecture can be distracting, try to be understanding. This is especially important if the student (or students) gives you a heads up on the matter and makes an effort to respect your authority.

CHAPTER 27
Impressing Office Staff & Your Boss

You never get a second chance to make a good first impression. Over the course of your first year of teaching, you want to make every effort to put your best foot forward. That is why you should be extra cautious to act in a professional manner at all times. In order to establish a good relationship with the office staff (who can make your life so much easier) and your boss, avoid the mistakes listed in this chapter.

MISTAKE 187
Avoiding extra work…

Throughout this book and the teachers who were interviewed have stated things such as, *"Do not get involved in campus politics"* or *"Do not get burned out."* However, you still need to be "true to your school," so to speak. You cannot dodge school events, even if somehow they do not involve you or your students. You cannot avoid all extracurricular activities, fundraisers, and other events and expect to be viewed positively by your employer.

While you do not need to volunteer or work yourself into the ground, it is smart to attend social events, eat lunch with your colleagues, and stop for small talk now and then. Additionally, if you can help a teacher out from time to time, you will find it easier to ask them for help if you ever need it. You are part of a team and need to prove yourself to be a valuable member.

MISTAKE 188
Not being considerate when using copiers and office equipment...

You are going to need to make copies, send faxes, and use other front-office equipment as much as any other teacher. Just be sure that you are considerate while doing so. Follow whatever rules and procedures your school has for use of office equipment and pay attention to other people who may be waiting in line for use of equipment. If you have a lot of copies to make, let someone with a short stack move ahead of you. And try not to ask any of the office staff to move a huge stack of work for you.

MISTAKE 189
Being overly defensive if a student complains about you...

If a student does file a complaint about you, defend yourself through documentation and approach the situation in a professional manner. Being overly defensive, argumentative, or emotional when speaking to your boss about an accusation against you will not help your case. Remain calm and reasonable and you can get your boss on your side, defending you to the parent or student. Any other approach and you might find yourself facing off against both the parent and administration.

MISTAKE 190

Taking too many sick days...

As you make every effort to create a good impression with your boss, you should know that taking too many days off will not accomplish this goal. While sick days cannot be helped, do not take days off without good cause. Of course, you do not want to go to school and give an entire class of children a bad case of the flu, but work hard to maintain good health (get a flu shot, take your vitamins, etc.).

MISTAKE 191

Not having a positive attitude...

One of the easiest ways to impress and improve relationships with your superiors and colleagues is the maintenance of a positive attitude and demeanor. All professions have their own set of challenges, especially teaching. However, if you approach your workload in a positive manner and are receptive of responsibilities or requests, you will quickly paint yourself as a reliable and preferred employee.

MISTAKE 192

Going over someone's head...

If you mistakenly bypass someone for a simple maintenance request or purposefully skip over someone you know is in your chain-of-command, you will definitely ruffle someone's feathers. While the situation may come up where this is necessary, do so with great caution.

MISTAKE 193

Not taking proper initiative...

I have gone over the importance of asking for help from your colleagues and superiors. However, a quick way to alienate yourself is to earn a reputation of not taking proper initiative. There is a time and a place to ask for help; however, running to your superiors with every minor technical or personal problem will not gain you any favor. Listening to and observing more experienced professors and really striving to be seen as competent and mature will help you to be taken more seriously.

MISTAKE 194

Not branching out...

Even though as a professor you have a specified area of interest and skill sets, it is important to use your position in an academic environment to your advantage. I have mentioned that, as teachers, we are always learning; however, as professors, this is a unique opportunity where you are actually being paid to attend school. At no other point in an education does this occur. Branch out and talk to professors in other fields and departments. Even if you have no personal interest in their subject matter, what you may learn can benefit your students or earn you a few friends in a different area which will diversify your knowledge as a whole.

MISTAKE 195

Complaining about the classes you are assigned to teach...

New teachers will often be assigned to the least desirable classes. If this conflicts with your idea of instructing the next generation of business leaders and scientists, do not make your dissatisfaction known. Even if you feel you are the best qualified to teach more advanced classes, you might still need to work your way into those roles. After all, teaching students who want to be in college is often more pleasurable than teaching those who will barely be able to graduate, but they are equally important. Do your best in whatever classes you are assigned to lead and eventually you will receive your more ideal courses.

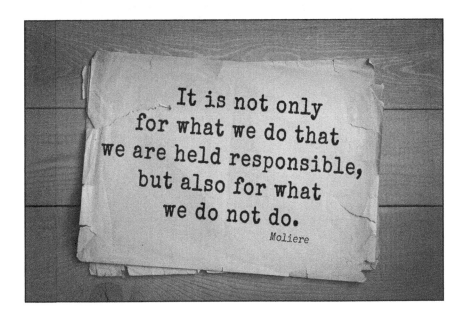

It is not only for what we do that we are held responsible, but also for what we do not do.

Moliere

CHAPTER 28
Final Thoughts

A great deal of this book has been dedicated to flooding you with awful mistakes you can make in your first year of teaching that could leave a bad impression on your students, your colleagues, or your superiors. I do not want to conclude this book without reminding you that your job does not have to be miserable or nothing but stress. You can have fun as a teacher and in the end, I hope you find it to be a highly fulfilling profession. Consider these final mistakes to avoid to make sure you still find some joy in what you do.

MISTAKE 196
Not smiling...

Do not forget to smile. Even if you are having a bad day, try to remember to smile at your students. When you see them smile back, it will lift your spirits and improve your mood. As much as you want to be firm with your students in terms of rules and classroom policies, that does not mean you need to appear to be in a dour mood all the time. Go ahead and let them see you smile; it will do both you and them some good.

MISTAKE 197

Not being warm and friendly...

While it is important to remain professional with your students, do not feel like you need to maintain a distant, aloof, or cold demeanor. Let yourself be warm and friendly with your students and you will probably have an easier time teaching them. You want them to feel comfortable approaching you with questions or asking for help, as that will help you get better results. If you act distant, they might not come to you. Find a way to be friendly and kind while maintaining appropriate levels of professionalism and classroom management and you will set yourself up for a successful first year.

MISTAKE 198

Not making friends among your coworkers...

If things work out, you will be working with these people for years to come and you should have a friendly relationship with your coworkers. While you want to keep your personal problems away from work, do not be afraid to consider yourself friends with your coworkers. Working in a school is the same as working in any corporate environment – enjoy the company of your colleagues, but remain professional at all work-related events.

MISTAKE 199

Not having any fun...

As strange as it might sound, failing to have any fun during your first year of teaching would be a terrible mistake. You will burn out and probably not want to return for another year whether you get an offer or not. Like I said in the introduction, teaching is one of the most difficult professions to work in – if you cannot enjoy it, you should not be doing it.

BIBLIOGRAPHY

"About Us." About Us. Ed. Scholastic News Editors. Scholastic News, 1996. Web. 27 Oct. 2016. <http://election.scholastic.com/about-us/>.

Burruss, Jill D. and Kaenzig, Lisa, "Introversion: The Often Forgotten Factor Impacting the Gifted," Virginia Association for the Gifted Newsletter. 1999 Fall 21 (1).

Fitzgerald, F. Scott, "My Lost City, Personal Essays, 1920-1940." Edited by James L.W. West III. Cambridge University Press, Cambridge, UK, 2005.

Flaherty, Colleen, "Trigger Unhappy." **www.insidehighered.com**. April 14, 2014.

Lattman, Peter, "The Origins of Justice Stewart's 'I Know it When I See It,'"LawBlog at The Wall Street Journal Online. December 31, 2014.

Lucier, Kelci, "Can a Student Date a Professor? You've Heard Rumors, But…What's the Deal?," **http://collegelife.about.com**.

Hembrooke, Helene and Geri Gay, "The Laptop and the Lecture: The Effects of Multitasking in Learning Environments," Journal of Computing in Higher Education. Vol. 15(1), Fall 2003.

Mason, D.A. & Good, T.L. "Effects of two-group and whole-class teaching on regrouped elementary students' mathematics achievement," *American Educational Research Journal*, vol. 30, pp. 328-360, 1993.

Orange, Carolyn, "25 Biggest Mistakes Teachers Make and How to Avoid Them, 2nd Ed." Corwin Press, Thousand Oaks, CA, 2008.

Reporter, Daily Mail. "Teachers 'watched Boy, 6, Slip on Snow Then Forced Him to Crawl Back to Class with a Broken Leg'" Mail Online. Associated Newspapers, 05 Jan. 2012. Web. 27 Oct. 2016.

Rockmore, Dan, "The Case for Banning Laptops in the Classroom," *The New Yorker*, June, 2014.

Rosenberg, Alyssa, "How trigger warnings could really work," *The Washington Post*. February 12, 2015.

Silverman, Linda, "What We Have Learned About Gifted Children," **www.gifteddevelopment.com** (2014).

Schuman, Rebecca, "Hands Off Your Grad Students! Yes, you're consenting adults. But you're harming your department, your discipline, and mentors everywhere." **www.slate.com** July 6, 2014.

Stein, Nathaniel, "Leaded! Harvard's Grading Rubric," *The New York Times*, December 14, 2013.

Strauss, Valerie, "Harvard College's median grade is an A-, dean admits," *The Washington Post*, December 4, 2013.

CONTRIBUTORS

Bill Hayes

Retired Teacher
& Department Head,
Leesburg High School

Brandy Mayer

Clerk of Courts,
New Orleans

David Allan West

Systems Administrator,
University of Florida

Greg Cumbaa

Manager, Technical Theatre,
Paul P. Williams Fine Arts
Center Theaters,
Lake Sumter Community College

Hollis Townsend

Director of Technology,
Support & Operations,
Young Harris College

Jill Mackavey

Professor,
Laban Institute of
Movement Studies,
Lesley University

Michael Grigsby

Senior Fiber Engineer,
General Dynamics

Sara Razaire

Volusia County Schools

Shay-Anne Matthews

Former Teacher,
Tavares Christian School

Shannon Bow O'Brien

Lecturer,
University of Texas, Austin

Steve Elcan

Regional Sales Director,
Oracle

AUTHOR BIOGRAPHY

Kimberly Sarmiento is a writer, researcher, and educator who currently leverages a background as a college professor and journalist to provide readers with advice on teaching, career management, and self-marketing. As an instructor, she developed  and led undergraduate courses such as *American Federal Government and Political Parties and Interest Groups* at Cameron University.

Ms. Sarmiento is a graduate from the University of Florida with a Master's in Political Science and a Bachelor's in Journalism. Over the course of her career, she has written for three regional newspapers, authored two books and several blogs on career management, and worked with hundreds of clients on the development of customized résumés and cover letters.

Recently, Ms. Sarmiento has been engaged on a volunteer basis to provide advice to teens on how they can translate high school experience into résumé content for the job market or college admissions. In her spare time, she enjoys going to theme parks with her children and reading.

INDEX

Made in the USA
Middletown, DE
01 June 2022

66491149R00157